CREATIVE VISION
and
INNER REALITY

© 2012 Shang Shung Publications
Località Merigar
58031 Arcidosso (GR)
Italy
www.shangshungpublications.org
info@shangshunginstitute.org

Cover design by Kasia Skura, Deniss Berezovsky
Inside book design by Daniel Zegunis

Cover photo by Chogyal Namkhai Norbu, 1982.
© Shang Shung Institute. All rights reserved.

ISBN 978-88-7834-124-1

CREATIVE VISION
and
INNER REALITY

EASING THE BEGINNER'S WAY:
THE ESSENTIAL POINTS *of*
CREATION AND COMPLETION

JAMGÖN KONGTRUL LODRÖ THAYE

Translated, introduced, and annotated by
ELIO GUARISCO

Shang Shung
Publications

Contents

Epigraph	7
Acknowledgments	9
Translator's Introduction	11
Jamgön Kongtrul Lodrö Thaye, the Author	11
This Text	19
Essence of the Creation Phase	22
Practice of the Creation Phase and Its Preliminaries	23
Essence of the Completion Phase	28
Practice of the Completion Phase	29
Beauty of the Advice	33

Creative Vision and Inner Reality

The Root Texts	35
I. Easing the Beginner's Way: The Essential Points of Creation and Completion (*lam zhugs kyi gang zag las dang po pa la phan pa'i bskyed rdzogs kyi gnad bsdus*)	37
II. Advice to Lhawang Tashi (*lha dbang bkra shis la gnang ba'i zhal gdams*)	75
Bibliography	81
Notes	91
Index of Tibetan and Sanskrit Terms	123

Epigraph

External things are mind's apparitions.
Like the moon's reflection on the surface of a pond,
That which is just an apparition is not real,
The perceiver of the apparition too is unreal.
Remain in that state of irreality free from any concept,
Nondual awareness and natural bliss will manifest.
In that state, existence as a condition has never come into being
And everything is the perfect mandala of your own true nature.

Shantigupta

Acknowledgments

I HAVE INCLUDED HERE another text by Jamgön Kongtrul Lodrö Thaye. I found these four folios of advice from the Great Kongtrul one cold winter night in a book that had been kindly loaned to me by the precious teacher, the Venerable Bokhar Rinpoche, during my stay at his monastery in Mirik near Darjeeling. The advice was inspiring and direct, and I felt it strongly as a blessing and counsel. These two pieces of heartfelt advice from an incomparable master are like luminous jewels that suddenly shine forth from an old coffer as one stumbles in the darkness.

I give profound thanks to Chögyal Namkhai Norbu for his assistance in editing the Tibetan texts that I used in this book and for clarifying crucial points. Moreover, I wish to thank Nancy Simmons, the English editor of the Ka-Ter Translation Project, for the generous use of her ever-present skills, Steven Landsberg for his appreciated work on the first draft, and Ingrid McLeod, my valued friend and companion in translation of some years, for her precious collaboration with "Advice to Lhawang Tashi."

Elio Guarisco
Sonada, India
January 2007

Translator's Introduction

Jamgön Kongtrul Lodrö Thaye, the Author

Jamgön Kongtrul Lodrö Thaye was an amazing scholar and realized being. He was born in eastern Tibet in 1813, the son of Yungdrung Tendzin, an illustrious master of the ancient Khyungpo clan,[1] whose descendants included outstanding masters of the Buddhist tradition such as Milarepa,[2] Khyungpo Naljor,[3] and the first Karmapa Tüsum Khyenpa,[4] as well as exemplary masters of the Bön tradition[5] such as tertön Loden Nyingpo[6] and Sharza Trashi Gyaltsen.[7]

A child of exceptional intelligence, Kongtrul had numerous visionary experiences and proclaimed with certainty to other children that he was an emanation of Guru Padmasambhava.[8] Kongtrul trained in the Bön tradition under his adoptive father and Yungdrung Phüntsog, the yogin of Tharde, who lived in a hermitage close to Kongtrul's native area. By the age of eight Kongtrul was proficient in the rites of Bön and familiar with the complete Bön pantheon. His wide range of interests included spirituality, art, religious dance, and medicine. As a precocious adolescent, he was able to identify all medicinal herbs and minerals, and later he became one of the most skilled physicians and alchemists in Tibet.

When Kongtrul was at the summer residence of the governor of Derge,[9] he met Jigme Losal, a teacher at Shechen Nyingma monastery[10] who was greatly impressed both by Kongtrul's knowledge and his ability to express it. Jigme Losal advised Kongtrul's patron to send him to study at Shechen under the great master Gyurme Thutob Namgyal.[11] At Shechen, Kongtrul received the transmissions of the teachings and practices of the Nyingma school as well as the secular sciences. It was there, in 1832, that Kongtrul received full ordination as a Buddhist monk by Thutob Namgyal according to the transmission of the Vinaya[12] found in eastern Tibet, a tradition shared by Nyingma and Gelug schools.

During the same year Kongtrul made a pilgrimage to the sacred place of Senge Namdzong with the Nyingma teacher Kunzang Sang Ngag. Along the way, the path became snowbound and they were unable to eat or rest for an entire day. When they finally reached a large slab of rock where they could rest, Kongtrul's teacher said, "If one looks directly at the mind when overcome by fatigue and hunger, one will perceive the mind essence just as it is." While they sat together in silence, Kongtrul had a direct and indescribable experience of the mind's essence. "Even later in my life," he wrote in his autobiography, "there was nothing to add or develop with respect to the essence I had seen."

During his first years as a monk, Kongtrul received instructions related to the *kama* and *terma* traditions.[13] He did several retreats, and countless signs manifested both in his dreams and waking state indicating his close spiritual affinity with Guru Padmasambhava and his teaching.

In 1883 Kongtrul was forcibly transferred from Shechen monastery by his patron, Tsephel of Khangsar, and taken to Palpung, the largest Kagyü monastery in eastern Tibet.[14] This sudden change, however, did not seem to have a detrimental effect upon him, and in his biography he remarks that on his journey to Palpung, snow fell and other auspicious signs appeared.

On the first day of the tenth lunar month of that year, Kongtrul met for the first time the ninth Situ, Pema Nyinje,[15] who would be his principal Kagyü teacher. Wöngen Trulku[16] insisted that Kongtrul take his ordination again according to the transmission of the Vinaya tradition[17] found in western Tibet followed in the Karma Kagyü and Sakya schools. Although this was an unorthodox request, Kongtrul accepted it.

By the age of thirty, Kongtrul had received teachings and transmissions from more than sixty masters representing all the different schools and esoteric lineages in Tibet. When his reputation began to spread, the Palpung authorities prevented the Derge government from removing Kongtrul in the same way they themselves had taken him from Shechen. They managed to do this by recognizing him as the incarnation of a learned monk, Bamteng Trulku, who had acted as the attendant of the previous Situ. As Bamten Trulku was from the region of Kongpo,[18] the newly recognized lama came to be called Kongtrul (the incarnation from Kongpo).

Although Kongtrul had acquired the title of an incarnate master in this way, it was not an undeserved title. In fact, Gyurme Thutob Namgyal had already proclaimed him to be an incarnation of the great translator Vairochana and later, many masters, such as Jamyang Khyentse Wangpo,[19] came to regard him as an incarnation of a number of previous realized beings, both Indian and Tibetan, beginning with Ananda (the Buddha's cousin), Aryadeva,[20] Khyungpo Naljor, Taranatha,[21] Terdag Lingpa,[22] and others. In any case, beyond these recognitions, throughout his life Kongtrul revealed himself to be an unequaled scholar and accomplished master.

At Palpung, Kongtrul progressed rapidly to become a foremost authority on all subjects of Buddhist studies and practice, and at the same time the receptacle of countless teachings that other masters showered upon him. Kongtrul practiced all the methods he was taught, one after the other, pursuing inner realization and invariably experiencing wonderful portents in dreams. He frequently dreamed of Guru

Rinpoche and of actually being Guru Rinpoche himself. He also had countless dreams containing prophetic indications.

A few years after he entered Palpung, the main seat of the Kagyü school in eastern Tibet, Kongtrul developed a strong affiliation with the Kagyü and his attraction to the ancient Nyingma tradition diminished. Soon, however, he recognized that this attitude was an obstacle and his affinity with the ancient tradition manifested again in dreams. Some of these dreams revealed to him the location of hidden treasure teachings or *terma*.

In 1839, Kongtrul met Jamyang Khyentse Wangpo for the first time, received transmission, and developed great faith in him. When Kongtrul entered his first traditional three-year retreat, he was interrupted after a year and a half: the fourteenth Karmapa Thegchog Dorje[23] was visiting Palpung monastery and had asked to be taught Sanskrit, and Kongtrul was deemed the right person to be his tutor. In 1842 when he was almost thirty, Kongtrul managed to extricate himself from outside demands on his time and attention. After an initial refusal, Situ Pema Nyinje finally granted him permission to recommence his three-year retreat. He constructed a small hut on the power site of Tsadra Rinchen Trag.[24] This hermitage remained his principal residence for the rest of his life and eventually became a three-year retreat center under his direction. It was also here that Kongtrul composed his literary works.

Kongtrul passed his life meditating, teaching, and writing, living most of the time in retreat. Realizing the pivotal role he had in the preservation and transmission of countless methods to achieve realization, he demonstrated a perfect balance between a contemplative and an active life. Poverty was his chosen close companion for many years, and unlike most teachers of his day, he preferred to live without attendants. Only his mother and, after the mother's death, his niece shared his residence and helped with household chores.

On one occasion, when performing a tantric feast,[25] he beheld in a waking vision the face of Guru Rinpoche as large as a mountain and thereupon recognized the natural state of mind wherein nothing is to be confirmed or rejected.

Kongtrul traveled widely in eastern Tibet, revitalizing the spirituality of the monasteries and retreat places and educating monks and laypersons by giving countless teachings, empowerments, transmissions, and instructions on methods for realization. He never kept the money and gifts given to him, but always offered them to Situ Pema Nyinje.

From Jamyang Khyentse Wangpo, Kongtrul frequently received teachings and empowerments of all traditions, particularly on the three series of Dzogchen,[26] the transmissions of Marpa,[27] and various Sakya lineages. In turn, Kongtrul conferred the teachings, empowerments, longevity rites, and blessings that Khyentse Wangpo requested from him. Although they were both student and teacher of each other, Kongtrul sought from Khyentse advice on all matters, especially after the passing of Situ Pema Nyinje.

With Khyentse, Chogyur Lingpa[28] and several other masters, Kongtrul played a vital role in the nineteenth-century cultural and spiritual renaissance known as the *rime*[29] or nonsectarian movement that took place in eastern Tibet. Kongtrul was the saintly scholar who had countless transmissions and the capacity to put everything into writing, Chogyur Lingpa was the unhindered mystic, and Khyentse Wangpo was the inspirational force behind the renaissance. Kongtrul stated in his autobiography that by merely invoking Guru Rinpoche, Khyentse Wangpo would encounter ancient masters and tertöns in visions and dreams, receiving teachings from them, many of which had been lost.

Kongtrul, Khyentse Wangpo, and Chogyur Lingpa were unbiased in their approach to the teachings in that their interests were not directed exclusively toward the tradition to which they belonged. They collected, practiced, taught, and wrote down the teachings of every transmission lineage included in the vast array of Buddhist teachings. In so doing they were able to preserve, revitalize, and propagate all the transmissions at a time when a real danger existed that these lineages could disappear due to the widespread sectarianism that imbued the spiritual environment. These masters obviously had a tremendous impact on the spirituality of Tibet, and the results of their efforts to preserve the teachings resonate even to this day.

Throughout the period of this revival, these three masters gave their primary attention to the Dzogchen and *terma* teachings that were closely related to their personal practice. In fact, the longest of Kongtrul's many writings and compilations is *The Treasury of Precious Termas*,[30] which contains more than sixty large volumes of important *terma* cycles. In his *Treasury of Knowledge*[31] he states that he considers the Dzogchen system as the peak of all the paths to realization taught in the sutras and tantras.

The all-embracing attitude of Kongtrul and his colleagues clearly was not intended to merge the various Tibetan traditions into a single school, but to prevent sectarianism, that is, the sense of belonging exclusively to a particular tradition and the belief in the validity of only one system. It is easy for a limited intellect that knows only a single philosophical presentation, only one secret oral instruction, or only one system of meditation to fall prey to the idea that one's own path is the only correct way. Respect and openness can free the mind from bias or partiality and lead to an understanding of the usefulness, scope, and particular qualities of all spiritual traditions. This benefit alone outweighs the risk of confusion when confronted with different and sometimes variant teachings.

In 1855, Chogyur Lingpa officially recognized Kongtrul as a *tertön* or discoverer of *terma* or hidden treasure teachings, and afterwards both Chogyur Lingpa and Khyentse Wangpo requested Kongtrul to participate in rites related to the discovery of their *termas*. Kongtrul thus became a holder of their *termas* as well. When Kongtrul decided to compile old and new *termas,* later named *The Treasury of Precious Termas,* he sought the advice of Khyentse Wangpo, who encouraged him to do so. To empower the undertaking of such a compilation, Kongtrul engaged in several retreats, until in 1856 he had numerous auspicious dreams including one in which he found precious pills belonging to Vimalamitra[32] and Yeshe Tsogyal[33], the Tibetan consort of Guru Rinpoche. He also dreamed that he was seated on a throne reading a scripture written in silver that contained exceptional instructions. He dreamed of the dawning of the sun and moon together and of receiving a blessing from a *terma* vase that Chogyur Lingpa had discovered, and so forth. He took all these signs as indications that it was time to begin composing the work. After the compilation of each part, Kongtrul was requested by incarnate masters and meditators to confer the empowerments and transmissions included in it. Rapidly, these transmissions were propagated throughout the communities of practitioners in eastern Tibet and they developed like no other teaching has since then.

Despite the influence Kongtrul exerted in the spiritual environment in eastern Tibet, at the age of sixty-one, after he had composed many of the works that had earned him great esteem, and after he had become the teacher of countless incarnate lamas and spiritual practitioners of eastern Tibet, a few partisan monks from Palpung monastery initiated a dispute to discredit him and Lama Wöngen. They held both Kongtrul and Lama Wöngen responsible for grievances of the young incarnation of the late Situ Pema Nyinje, probably doing so because they could not tolerate Kongtrul's broad vision and all-embracing attitude toward all teachings, especially those of the ancient tradition. Finally the senior administrator of Derge county, Tsering Töndrub, was asked to investigate the matter, and ultimately the allegations were found to be unjustified.

When the dispute came to an end, it was decided that Kongtrul would remain in his own hermitage and Lama Wöngen would take up residence in Drenthang. After some time, the Situ incarnation took responsibility for the dispute that forced Kongtrul from Palpung for fourteen years, and offered his apologies. By the end of Kongtrul's life, most of the great masters and incarnate teachers of the nineteenth century had become his disciples.

Kongtrul died in his eighty-seventh year on Thursday, December 28, 1899. He was an extremely prolific writer, having compiled more than ninety volumes on the theory and practice of the Dzogchen, Nyingma, Kadam, Sakya, Kagyü, and Bön traditions.[34] His major works are traditionally known as *The Five Great Treasuries*,[35] a name that Khyentse gave to the work when he saw the first draft of the first of the five, entitled *The Treasury of Knowledge*. His title was prophetic because he foresaw that Kongtrul would compose four other works. In addition, Kongtrul wrote texts explaining rites, provided words of advice for students, and wrote philosophical exegeses. He discussed Indian and Chinese astrology, traditional Tibetan medicine, grammar, and other subjects.

Kongtrul's huge literary output gives the impression that he spent most of his life writing. In fact, most of his life was dedicated to meditation retreats and teaching others. He said that he wrote his works often in the intervals between his meditations. The totality of Kongtrul's life, the depth of his practice, and his comprehensive writings are amazingly difficult to fathom and leave us with a feeling of wonder and disbelief that such a great being could have ever existed.[36]

This Text

The short text by Jamgön Kongtrul entitled *Easing the Beginner's Way: The Essential Points of Creation and Completion That Help the Beginner on the Path* is advice that he composed at the request of Karma Palden, an attendant to the fourteenth Karmapa.

The text is neither a traditional commentary on the two phases of a specific tantra nor a general explanation of the highest tantra. It is advice that contains Kongtrul's own experiential understanding of these two phases. That he dictated this advice when he was only twenty-seven years of age reveals the depths he had fathomed not only of tantric practice but also of the highly esoteric traditions of Mahamudra[37] and Dzogchen. In fact, this text is invaluable for practitioners because of the interpolation of practical advice drawn from these two traditions.

A summary of Kongtrul's treatment of the two phases found in the eighth section of his *Treasury of Knowledge*[38] is helpful as an introduction to the meaning of the two phases of the highest Yogatantra.

Tantra was first introduced in Tibet during the early propagation that occurred in the eighth century with the original translations of the tantras of that century that formed the basis of the ancient or Nyingma tradition. This tradition classifies all the ways to realization in nine vehicles: the mundane vehicle of humans and gods; the vehicle of Listeners (*shravaka*) and Solitary Realizers (*pratyeka*); the vehicle of the Bodhisattvas (*mahayana*); the Action Tantra (*kriya*); the Tantra of Both (*ubhaya*), the Tantra of Union (*yoga*); the Great Yoga (*mahayoga*); Anuyoga; and Atiyoga or Dzogchen.

These nine vehicles are grouped into three sets of three. The first set of three encompasses the vehicles that stem from Sutra or the discourses of the Buddha that guide one toward liberation by means of the relinquishing of actions and emotions which are the cause of suffering. These three vehicles are therefore known as the way of liberation from the source of suffering.

The second set of three represents the outer form of Tantra. In these tantras the practitioner follows ritual practices such as ablution and strict cleanliness, similar to the customs of the Brahmins, proponents of the Vedas. Hence, these three tantras are known as the way resembling Vedic austerity.

The last set of three are the inner tantras that conclusively establish, without requiring any specific way of conduct, the knowledge that everything animate and inanimate, the nature of the mind, is the indivisibility of the two superior truths.[39] These yogas are therefore the skillful methods whereby all phenomena are governed within the state of total sameness. Thus they are designated as the way of the governing method.

The second propagation of Buddhism began with the new translations of the tantras (tenth and eleventh centuries) made by Rinchen Zangpo and others. The schools that developed from these translations are known as Sarma or new schools. These schools classified the tantras into four divisions consisting of the Action Tantra, Conduct Tantra (*charya*), Tantra of Union (*yoga*) and Highest Tantra of Union (*mahanuttara yogatantra*).

While Anuyoga and Atiyoga are exclusive to the ancient tradition and are not found in any other Tibetan schools, the Nyingma Mahayoga and the Anuttaratantra of the new schools largely converge on the same view and manner of practice. A proof that substantiates this similarity is that both traditions contain tantras such as the *Guhyasamaja* and the *Chandraguhyatilaka*.

In the *Guhyasamaja* it is explained that tantra (or continuity) denotes the awakened mind (*bodhichitta*), the ever perfect (*samantabhadra*) without beginning or end that has the nature of luminous clarity. It is continuous in that from time without beginning until the attainment of enlightenment, it is present without any interruption.

Such tantra consists of three aspects: cause, method, and result. The tantra of the cause denotes the sky-like natural condition of one's own mind that is the unchanging union of natural awareness and bliss that manifests as the two mental states of calm and movement. As it is the fundamental stuff of awakening, it is called the tantra of the cause. This is also known as the essence of enlightenment, Samantabhadra, reality as it is, or the original Buddha.

The tantra of the method in a broad sense refers to all possible aspects of the path, but mainly to the two phases of the Anuttaratantra and its branches that are applied after initiation. The contributory condition for awakening, it is called the tantra of the method.

The tantra of the result is the accomplishment experienced when the tantra of the cause, freed from all adventitious stains, transforms, causing one to manifest in the state of full awakening which becomes a source of benefit for others as well as for oneself. This awakening that is thus the fulfillment of great benefit is called the tantra of the result.

This means that all our vision is produced by the inconceivable force of our past actions. This vision, however, is illusory, just like the falling hair seen by a person with cataracts. Although it seems to be separate from us, it is not, because it arises as a result of beginningless ignorance. Even when our vision seems very real, the ground from where it manifests, that is, the mind that is natural luminous clarity, is present without the tarnish of habitual tendencies that create illusion. This mind of luminous clarity is the causal tantra.

Relying on the esoteric instructions of an authentic master, one acquires familiarity with the understanding that whatever appears is the very essence of luminous clarity in which there is nothing to be eliminated or added. Practitioners who are not capable of this understanding apply methods whereby all vision is freely enjoyed as the manifestation of the mandala of the deities. Having approached the wisdom of luminous clarity in either of these two ways, one stabilizes the practice of acquaintance with this wisdom so that it becomes continuous like the current of a river. This is called the tantra of method.

As one develops familiarity in that way, although one's mind essence manifests freely in the form of all phenomena, since the stains of illusion are exhausted, the dualistic impressions are absent and mind essence is realized as the great wisdom. As this state is unaffected by even the slightest concept of subject and object duality, an awakened activity spontaneously manifests that completely and effortlessly fulfills all aspirations of sentient beings. This state of awakened activity is called the tantra of result.

Although numerous differences exist between the new schools and the ancient tradition, including deities, tantras, manners of practice, and styles of explanation, all the methods of the highest Yogatantra, Mahayoga, and Anuyoga consist of the two phases of creation and completion.

Essence of the Creation Phase

The phase of creation is artificial in the sense that yogins recreate the environment as the mandala and themselves as the deity by utilizing imagination and thought. This is accomplished through a series of gradual steps. Although this phase uses an artifice, for those who do not have a higher capacity, the phase of creation serves effectively to overcome ordinary vision and fixed concepts.

How is this done in the phase of creation? By visualizing the deity's form one prevents ordinary perception and fixation from arising.

Moreover, by realizing that the deity is without any true existence, ultimately one puts an end to grasping at the reality of the deity.

Through the path of sutra, one subdues emotions, the cause of suffering, and thereby simply prevents the result, the experience of suffering, from arising in the future. Through the path of mantra, from the beginning one transforms suffering, the impure vision itself, into a pure mandala so that the actual experience of suffering never occurs.

In the phase of creation one transcends ordinary vision by meditating on the clear vision of the deity's form. One overcomes ordinary human pride by cultivating pride in being a *heruka*.[40] Recognizing the mandala as a magical creation, one overcomes one's addiction to any reality.

The methods of visualization are many and can either be elaborate or simple. Generally speaking, they can be subsumed under four methods: instantaneous visualization, visualization from a seed syllable, a three-step visualization (moon, seed syllable, deity), and visualization through the five actual awakenings.[41] With regard to these methods, it is said that practitioners of weak or mediocre faculties should visualize the deity gradually, and those of sharp faculties should visualize the deity instantaneously.

Moreover, the phase of creation should be understood as a method for purifying, in general, ordinary birth, death, and the intermediate state, but in particular, for purifying birth.

Practice of the Creation Phase and Its Preliminaries

Three preliminaries are necessary before the main practice of the creation phase: first, an offering of food[42] to obstructing forces in order to appease them. Second, the visualization of the protection circle created in order to dispel adverse conditions. Third, for the common protection circle, the ground, the enclosing fence, and the tent are imagined as made of *vajras*;[43] for the uncommon protection circle, the ten wrathful deities are visualized as arranged on the spokes of a ten-spoked golden wheel[44] that annihilates all obstructing forces.

To establish favorable conditions, the two accumulations of merit and wisdom are gathered. In order to accumulate merits, offerings are made to the master visualized in the form of the deity. As a means of self purification, the sevenfold service is recited, accompanied by the altruistic resolve to awaken.[45]

Wisdom is gathered by meditating on emptiness while reciting the emptiness mantra. Through familiarity with the view that recognizes with certainty that all phenomena are primordially devoid of intrinsic essence, one recollects the unborn emptiness beyond conceptuality.

After these preliminaries, the first step of the main practice of the creation phase is the visualization of the celestial palace, the residence of the deities. The celestial palace can be manifested in several ways: from the letter *bhrum*, from a wheel, or from the dissolving of Vairochana. The palace is visualized as a luminous and transparent abode having the nature of wisdom. With four sides and four gates, it is ornamented by eight pillars and four archways, adorned with loops and pendants, banners, and yak tail fans.[46]

The visualization also includes the charnel grounds.[47] Imagined outside the celestial palace, each charnel ground is characterized by various elements: a special tree, a *yaksha*[48] on the tree, a guardian of a direction, a *naga*,[49] a peculiar cloud in the sky above, a mountain, and a stupa.[50] Moreover, the charnel grounds are populated by many kinds of birds, wild animals, fragrant flowers, fearsome apparitions, skeletons, and corpses. There are also temples, monasteries, hermitages, and ponds. All sorts of beings, both human and nonhuman, wander in these charnel grounds. Among the humans are yogins and yoginis, displaying different moods, some dancing, some singing, some drinking liquor, and so forth.[51]

Within the celestial palace one also visualizes a seat consisting of a lotus, sun, and moon for all deities of the mandala. One then creates the entire circle of the resident deities: first the main male and female deity in union and then the deities of the retinue. There are various ways in which the main deity is created but the most common is through the five actual awakenings.

One imagines that above a lotus seat, from the vowels of the Sanskrit alphabet, a moon disk arises, and from the consonants, a sun disk. Between the sun and moon is the symbol of the deity, marked with its seed syllable from which light emanates and reabsorbs. All these elements merging together create the manifestation of oneself as the complete body of the deity.

The moon symbolizes the white vital essence, the sun symbolizes the red vital essence, and the seed syllable symbolizes the consciousness in the intermediate state. The merging of these elements into one corresponds to the moment of conception, and the full manifestation of the divine body corresponds to birth from a womb.

In some tantras the main deity visualized at the beginning of the *sadhana*[52] is called the causal Vajradhara. This main deity then coalesces into a sphere of luminous seminal essence and again emerges as a form after being invoked with melodious words of request by four female deities of the mandala who symbolize the four immeasurable aspirations: equanimity, compassion, love, and joy. From that moment they are referred to as the fruitional Vajradhara. Some tantras dispense with this phase of transmutation and specify that the main male and female deities are created only once.

Also, the deities of the retinue can be created in different ways: through the five actual awakenings, the three steps (moon, seed syllable, deity), or simply from a seed syllable. In most tantras the deities of the retinue are first visualized as being born from the womb of the consort of the main male deity and then, one by one, emerge to take their places in the mandala.

The placement of the three beings (pledge being, wisdom being, and contemplation being) follows, a step that is found in most *sadhanas*. The pledge being is the visualization of oneself as the deity of whom one has received the initiation through ritual steps and is also called the pledge deity. Depending upon the *sadhana*, the wisdom being can be visualized at the heart of the pledge deity, identical in color, face, and hands with the pledge deity, or as having a different form than the pledge deity. The wisdom being, representing the yogin's consideration of the real deity, can also be visualized as a symbol such as a *vajra* that has manifested from a seed syllable on a seat composed of lotus and sun, and so forth. The contemplation being is visualized as a seed syllable or symbol in the heart of the wisdom being. When the wisdom being is visualized in the form of a symbol, the contemplation being will be represented by the seed syllable. The establishing of the three beings may be done with regard to all the deities of the retinue or for the central deity alone.

The majority of tantric texts, at this point, also teach the consecration or empowerment of the sense organs. In most cases the consecration consists in visualizing deities in the sense organs that manifest from their seed syllable. In some *sadhanas* there is a three-step creation (that is, visualizing a moon, a syllable, and the transformation into the deity). In others it is explained that the deities are not visualized, but just their seed syllables are created with the mind. In addition to the visualization of the palace and the deities, the completion of the meditation requires the drawing of the wisdom *mandala*,[53] receiving the initiation, sealing oneself with the lord of the family,[54] tasting the nectar,[55] offering, and praising oneself as the deity. These steps are to be completed in the specified order.

At all times during the creation phase, one must recognize that the mandala of the deities that appears to the mind is a relative vision that has no true existence. With this knowledge, one must train in the contemplation that everything is like a magical creation. In the end, the form of the deity and the pride of being the deity must be perceived as wisdom whose essence is beyond any conceptual limit and whose unimpeded manifestation is empowered with bliss induced by different methods.

When weary of visualizing the deity, one recollects the real meaning of what is visualized.[56] As for the true meaning of the relative deity, all the aspects of the visualization are in a real sense the supreme qualities of enlightenment.

At the end of each session of meditation, one dissolves the visualization: the residence and resident deities are dissolved into oneself whereupon even the self gradually vanishes into luminous clarity. Again one reemerges from luminous clarity as the simple illusory form of the deity.

At this point one applies the methods of the eight yogas: mantra recitation, food offering made to the deities and elemental spirits, partaking of food and drink, sexual union with a qualified consort, the activities between sessions, sleep, awakening at dawn, and cleansing.

There are many distinct visualizations and methods of execution for these yogas, all to be practiced according to their respective instructions.

Essence of the Completion Phase

The nature of the completion phase is innateness, nonconceptuality, and totality. These three main characteristics of the completion phase are all present in the base, path, and result.

From the perspective of the base, for an ordinary being innateness is of two kinds: innateness as bliss arising from the melting[57] of the vital essence and innateness as the ultimate condition of existence. The bliss of melting refers to the four joys that arise during sexual union.[58] As to the innate condition of existence, the *Hevajra Tantra* states:[59]

> *Innateness as the real condition of existence*
> *Is the single reality that unifies all forms.*

This refers to the state of Vajrasattva, one's own primordial state, that has no beginning or end. It includes all animate and inanimate phenomena and exists beyond limitations of time. Thus it is termed innate. The characteristic of innateness itself is endowed with nonconceptuality. Totality, the third characteristic, means that which encompasses the body and all phenomena. Such a reality, represented by the completion phase, exists within the ordinary body of each individual and is not something that arises anew from it. Thus the body is considered the base, and reality is based or found in that. Consequently, such a reality can be made manifest by relying on the coarse body.

The completion phase of the base is also called unity, the indestructible condition, and the inseparability of emptiness and compassion. It is this ground of inseparability that is contemplated in the completion phase of the path. At the time of the result, it is this alone which is realized.

In regard to the path, the phase of completion must be initiated by working on the crucial points of the *vajra* body.[60] This is accomplished by forcing and binding the ordinary mind and ordinary wind energies that are the cause of various thoughts and concepts into the central channel. In brief, bliss and emptiness come about by absorbing mind and wind energy into the central channel.

The actual phase of completion occurs when one recognizes the innate condition of bliss, derived from the melting of the vital essences of one's body. Without depending on imagining in meditation, the nonconceptual yoga manifests as the self-appearing form of the deity in which emptiness and great bliss manifest simultaneously: this is a special aspect of the completion phase.

Practice of the Completion Phase

As to the actual practice, there are countless completion phase methods related to various tantras and to the secret instructions of *siddhas*.[61] These should be learned orally from a qualified master. All of these practices resemble each other in that they include three aspects:

1. The methods concentrate on the central channel of the body through visualization, *prana* practice, and *yantra* physical training[62] applied on the basis of the knowledge of the yoga of channels, winds, and vital essences.
2. The methods use the path of the wisdom consort, the method of another body for recognizing the four joys induced by passion, through the descent, withholding, reversal, and spread of the vital essence.

3. The methods induce the immutable bliss through the Mahamudra of empty form[63] beyond conceptualization and physical or verbal effort.

At the commencement of each practice of the completion phase, the channels, winds, and vital essences need to be readied with different techniques depending on whether one is following the father or mother tantras. The techniques of the father tantras focus mainly on *prana*. As the wind energy enters into the central channel, the four emptinesses appear one after the other, producing ever more subtle experiences. Known as empty, very empty, greatly empty, and totally empty, the four are related to experiences that correspond respectively to light, the diffusion of light, the culmination of light, and luminous clarity.[64]

The techniques of the mother tantras mainly work on the vital essence by activating the key points within the *vajra* body. First, when sufficient experience in visualizing one's body and channels[65] as totally empty and in the vase-like holding of the breath have been gathered, one applies the vital essence yoga.

The most important method in the vital essence yoga is known as inner heat.[66] In a system unique to the mother tantras, the inner heat of bliss is related to the dripping of the white vital essence from the crown of the head, the inner heat derived from the blazing A-stroke,[67] and the inner heat of no thought, which is the union of the previous two. As a result of igniting the inner fires and developing control over the winds, one experiences the four joys and the four emptinesses manifesting in union and realizes the result of the practice of inner fire.

Thus the body represented as channels, winds, and vital essences is the focus of the special tantric methods. The main channels are three: the *avaduthi* or central channel flanked by the *lalana* and *rasana* channels. In the new schools the *lalana* is the channel of the lunar vital essence located to the left of the central channel. The *rasana* is the channel of the solar vital essence located on the right side of the central channel.

In the unique perspective of the Ati Dzogchen tradition the *rasana* corresponds to the lunar essence located on the right side in men and on the left in women. The *lalana* corresponds to the solar essence, and is on the left side in men and on the right side in women. Among numerous channels classified in many ways, the principle ones are the thirty-two in which the vital essence of *bodhichitta* flows. The places where these channels concentrate their energy are called chakras, the principal four of which are at the crown, the throat, heart, and navel. Since the heart region, the seat of the mind, is the nucleus where everything is produced and reabsorbed, a tantrika focuses primarily upon that center.

There are five main wind energies: life-sustaining, ascending, fire-accompanying, downward-clearing, and pervading, each with its specific locations and functions.[68] In tantric techniques, the yogin mainly works with the upper and lower wind energies. During meditation the wind energies are employed in the *vajra* recitation[69] and the *prana* practices that accompany the various visualizations and methods of the completion phase.

Vital essences are of two kinds: the red vital essence derived from the mother, which has the nature of fire, and the white vital essence derived from the father, which has the nature of bliss. In actual practice, these are related to the navel chakra and the crown chakra respectively. At the navel or four fingers below the navel, the red vital essence is usually visualized as a tiny triangle of red fire, hot and blazing.[70] The white vital essence is visualized at the crown of the head as a white letter *ham* upside down. Through the interaction of these two during the inner heat practice, one experiences bliss.

Although father and mother tantras diverge at the commencement of the completion phase, they converge at the end with the three practices of the illusory body, clear light, and the state of union. In the practice of the illusory body, one really manifests as the mandala and the deities. In the practice of clear light, one enters the nondual essence of mind. In the practice of the state of union, the illusory body and clear light become totally inseparable, and thus one achieves the fruit of enlightenment.

A typical completion phase meditation could be described as follows: one meditates, for example, on the letter *hum* at the heart in between the sun and moon joined within the central channel. Alternatively, visualize a sphere of molten vital essence, white with a red hue, on the tip of the secret *vajra*. At the door of the senses visualize letters or spheres that prevent the flow of wind energies. Then imagine that at the navel the fire of inner heat blazes and its heat reaches the crown of the head and dissolves the letter *ham* which symbolizes the vital essence of bliss. The vital essence drips to the navel or heart where the fire blazes and you as the deity are consecrated with bliss. Then the two contemplations of viewing as a whole and subsequent destruction[71] are applied through which you repeatedly dissolve the universe, beings, and yourself as a means to enter the state of luminous clarity. Thus by alternating the arising of the deity and the dissolution into emptiness-luminous clarity, you achieve the realization of the state of union, which is the inseparability of Mind-*dharmakaya* and Body-*nirmanakaya*.[72]

The specific instructions are very detailed and should be learned from a qualified master. Once experience has been gained in these two phases, the practitioner must engage, secretly or openly, in either elaborate, unelaborate, or simple tantric activities.[73] These actions are the proximate cause for total realization. The aim of these activities, practicing with a consort or engaging in "crazy" behavior, is the experience of total equality and the state of bliss and emptiness.

With these methods even people with the lowest capacity can achieve greatness. Accordingly, the *Guhyasamaja* states:

Even beings who have committed great evils
such as the heinous crimes
will become realized through

this great ocean of the indestructible path,
the supreme way to realization.

BEAUTY OF THE ADVICE

It is my hope that the foregoing introduction may further the reader's appreciation of the extreme beauty and utility of Kongtrul's short text on the two phases. Although this text is entitled *Essential Points of Creation and Completion*, in reality it may be considered as profound advice for the practice of Mahamudra and Dzogchen. Many points discussed by Kongtrul are pertinent to those two systems, which represent the ultimate sense of all teachings. It is not necessary to discuss these points as they are strikingly clear and tangible for anyone interested in or practicing the path to the natural state. Without need for a detailed analysis, the reader can approach them as an awesome and beautiful snow peak that suddenly reveals itself to the climber as he or she reaches the summit of a mountain pass.

CREATIVE VISION
and
INNER REALITY

EASING THE BEGINNER'S WAY:
THE ESSENTIAL POINTS OF CREATION
AND COMPLETION

HOMAGE

I bow to Pema Nyinje Wangpo,[74]
An emanation inseparable from Padma Vajra[75] himself,
Who opens and reabsorbs a multitude of entries
    to the unconditioned,
Everlasting, ultimate contemplation of bliss and emptiness.

When the signs of degeneration[76] have fully manifested,
What is the use for an ordinary person like me to explain
    what is profound and vast?[77]
It is just a cause of weariness.
Nevertheless, my *vajra* brother[78] has requested me to do so;
And since it may be advice that benefits ignorant ones such as
    myself,
I will speak freely what comes to mind,
Relying solely on the blessing of the glorious master.

You have now obtained a rare and precious life.[79]
Not remaining an ordinary person, you have met the dharma;
And you have become a student of a master, a real buddha.
You have chosen the most profound essential teachings
And the finest of masters. That is sufficient!

At this moment while you still have the chance and all
    circumstances favor your practice,
Even if you are unable to benefit others,
At least practice to become self-reliant.

Otherwise, at the time of death, the moment of which is
    unpredictable,
Even the wealth of emperors is left behind and nothing
    but the teaching can help.
Your mind will trail after positive and negative actions
And you will not know what to do. Even regret will be
    of no use.
Therefore, from this second without postponing,
Exert yourself in the virtuous actions of the three doors.[80]

The only true foundation for practice is the wish to be free
    from habitual life.
The only approach is faith,
The main road is compassion,
And the only backbone is complete and assiduous training.
Indispensable to the practice are conscientiousness, presence,
    and awareness.[81]
Trust in the Precious Jewels[82] eliminates obstacles,
Devotion to the master enhances the practice,
And the master's instructions ensure that it is flawless.
All the essential points of practice are unified in the Three
    Roots.[83]
When the peaceful and wrathful mandalas
Arise as the master's display, this alone is sufficient!

Superior persons with the highest capacity who have trained in
    previous lives,
Those with perfect devotion, and saintly men are deemed
    supreme
And can behold the true nature of reality

Even without effort along the stages of the path.
All others should attend to the instructions of the exalted
 Nagarjuna,[84]
"Learning yields the fruit of reflection
And reflection gives rise to experiences of meditation,
 in that order."
If you ignore distractions and exert yourself continuously,
First, through the wisdom derived from learning,
You will understand the general characteristics of habitual life
 and freedom.
Through reflection you will overcome conspicuous grasping at
 illusory vision as real;
Through meditation you will gain decisive understanding of
 your own condition, and so on;
And in that way the former stages can result in the latter ones.
Lacking this process is only wishing for a result without
 a cause!
Thinking, "My practice of purification and gathering of
 merits[85] is the finest of any!"
Bemoaning the hardship of practice in which you lack decisive
 understanding,
Will not result in concrete experiential knowledge.
Without decisive knowledge, you remain in doubt,
And doubt is the single obstacle to the supreme realization.
When you arrive at real knowledge through learning, reflection,
 and meditation,
Even if someone were to say, "This meditation of yours will
 lead you to hell,"
You would not be intimidated as you have genuine
 knowledge.

The essential point of all the ways of practice taught by the
    Victorious One
Can be epitomized as a method to tame one's mind,
And the initial entry to mind training is the very wish
To be free from habitual life. This is indispensable!
If you have a genuine wish to go beyond usual life, your
    activities will be few;
If your activities are few, you are close to the state of
    nonaction.
When you realize nonaction, you have discovered the authentic
    condition,[86]
And there is no enlightenment other than that.

View, meditation, and conduct[87] can be distinguished in a
    multitude of ways,
But when subsumed in regard to one's own mind
The view is full conviction in the natural state,
Meditation is integrating the view in one's own condition,
Conduct is any action flavored by the view and meditation:
The result is said to be the authentic condition.

The very source of confusion
Is one's own mind grasping external vision as true.
Whether one meditates upon the creation or the completion
    phase,
Either one is just a method to overcome clutching at illusory
    vision as real.
If the obstinate habits of attachment and aversion are not
    changed,
Meditation is pointless and resembles a groundhog hibernating
    in its hole.

The names of the two phases define their characteristics:
The expansive creation phase is contrived and imaginary,[88]
The profound completion phase is natural and perfect.[89]
Similarly, they are conceptual and nonconceptual respectively.[90]
Since both of these phases, taught according to the greater or
    the lesser mental capacities of individuals,
Are surely the genuine intention of the Victorious One,
They cannot be differentiated in terms of better or worse.
The crucial point is to practice one or the other in keeping
    with one's own capacity.

On the way of mantra, which has many methods and no
    hardships,[91]
All actions of those with sharp faculties and great
    discrimination
Become the two accumulations of merit and wisdom,
And nothing in the slightest is meaningless.
However, this path is not within the reach of the ignorant with
    wrong views.

Through the crucial points of focused aspiration,
Little belief in anything as real,
Deep faith, appreciation, and trust in the path of method,[92]
The ordinary and the supreme attainments[93] will come more
    swiftly than an invited guest.

Everything is included in the two truths
Expressed in the infallible logical axioms:
"The relative truth is valid in relation to ignorance,
And the absolute truth is valid in relation to the ultimate
    nature."

If you understand that the two truths are indivisible like the
    reflection of the moon in water,[94]
You are close to the end of illusory vision.
It is true that enlightenment is achieved through both the
    indirect and direct paths,[95]
But there is the distinction that one is longer, the other, shorter.
For example, like going to the same destination, such as Lhasa,
By walking or by flying in the sky.
However, even if the path is short,
The profound special quality of the direct path will not
    manifest to a person of inferior capacity,
And such a one will remain in an ordinary condition.

Disdaining the lower without having reached the higher,
Proffering empty talk without regard for the law of causality,
One only pays lip service to the view and makes a fool of
    oneself.
Better that such a one keep to the gradual path!

Although the methods on the path entered, be it sutra
    or mantra,
Are similar in that both are vast and manifold,
They are different in that sutra practice, as the Omniscient
    One[96] said,
Is to do no evil whatsoever, to practice virtue, and to tame the
    mind;
While the mantra system consists of
Meditation on the two phases of creation and completion.
Since mind is the root of all phenomena, first of all
It is important to tame your mind,

Without this, familiarizing and actualizing,[97] making
   sacred objects,[98] and so on,
Even over several lifetimes, will not result in
   enlightenment.
Taming your mind means governing your emotions,
And the methods are said to be three: renunciation,
   transformation, and recognition.[99]
Renouncing emotions is the ordinary sutra path
In which attachment is abandoned through the antidote
   of meditation on repulsiveness,[100]
Hatred by meditation on loving kindness,
And ignorance by meditation on interdependence.[101]

Transforming emotions is the uncommon path of secret
   mantra.[102]
When attachment arises, you meditate on a deity such as
   Amitabha[103]
Or on a heruka[104] in union, and
The thought of attachment transforms into the meditational
   deity.[105]
And you deal with the other emotions in a similar way.

Recognizing the nature of the emotions is the supreme path.
When craving thoughts arise blindingly,
Looking directly at their nature, you find they vanish in their
   own condition,
And the Mahamudra of the indivisible bliss and emptiness,
Also known as discerning wisdom, arises.
From the beginning, there is nothing to abandon, accept,
Or transform because everything is your own mind.

Understand that apart from leaving mind essence in its
    natural state,
There is no other buddha mind.

The way of applying all three approaches in a single sitting
Is explained by Gyalwa Yangonpa:[106]
When you have thoughts of attachment,
Firmly resolve to renounce them as soon as they arise,
Thinking, "From now until enlightenment
I will cast off these ordinary thoughts of desire."
Then you imagine that any unbearable suffering
That sentient beings of the universe experience,
Distracted by ordinary thoughts of attachment,
As well as obstacles caused by such feelings
In the minds of practitioners of the teaching,
Are all instantly gathered into your own attachment,
Thereby liberating all beings from the bondage of the
    desiring mind.
Then thinking, "On the basis of my thoughts of attachment,
I shall meditate on the two phases
In order to establish all beings in the state of Vajradhara,"[107]
Instantly visualize yourself vividly as Heruka Chakrasamvara[108]
In union with his consort, complete with all ornaments.
Generally, to pursue a mundane thought of passion
While meditating on the forms of the deities is a mistake.
Focus your attention fully on the male deity
If the form of the female deity is too palpably vivid,
Since the risk exists that residual desire could surface
Resulting in the possible loss of semen,
And ultimately your mind would succumb to the power of
    attachment.

So visualize at the deity's heart upon a lotus and moon seat
Your root master, beautiful and majestic.
Invoke him sincerely again and again with these words:
"Empower me so that the passion-filled thoughts arising
  in my mind
May manifest as discerning wisdom."[109]
Then observe the essence of your mind sharply
As the inseparability of deity, master, and attachment.
Rest in meditation from the moment the emotion arises
Until the practice takes hold.
At the end, offer pure dedication and aspiration:
"By this virtue, may the passions and thoughts of attachment
Of all deluded sentient beings and of practitioners of the
  teaching,
That cause obstacles to the stages of realization and the path,
Be totally pacified, and may all beings realize the Mahamudra
  of bliss and emptiness.
Apply this method also to ignorance and hatred;
For the latter, meditation upon a peaceful deity is especially
  effective.

Primarily, the creation phase dispels ordinary illusory vision,
While the completion phase overcomes grasping illusory vision
  as real.
As long as creation and completion remain separate from one
  another,
Achievement of the true state of Vajradhara cannot happen in a
  single lifetime.
The union of creation and completion is the profound path,
But the actual union will not be discovered until the movement
  of thoughts arises as meditation,

So meditate alternating creation and completion,
And relinquish bogus union fabricated by the mind.

In applying the meditation of the creation phase,
You must have a general understanding of the basis,
The objects, the methods, and the results of purification.
The basis of purification is the eternal, unconditioned, expanse
  of the true nature of reality[110]
That is the essence of enlightenment equally present in all
  beings,[111]
A natural wisdom endowed with the qualities of the dimension
  of reality[112]
And the major and minor marks.[113]
Just like a sun obscured by clouds,
The essence of enlightenment is obscured by adventitious
  stains of illusion
formed by ignorance since time without beginning,
While its potential natural qualities are like the rays of the sun.
The effaceable noninherent stains — emotions, obscurations
  of knowledge, and Impediments to meditative absorption[114]
  — are like clouds,
Blots that are the objects to be purified.
The methods of purification consist in the many yogas of
  shape:[115]
Five actual awakenings,[116] four *vajras*,[117] and three rituals[118]
Which purify birth from a womb, from an egg,
From warmth and moisture; and instantaneous recollection of
  the deity which purifies miraculous birth.[119]
Although numerous variant explanations by scholars exist as to
  methods which purify these births,[120]
You should know that they are not contradictory.

Although the visualization of the deity from the beginning
    until the dissolution
Consistsof many sequential steps,
The basis of purification is the very essence of enlightenment,
And the objects to be purified are the illusions occurring
From the moment consciousness enters the womb, through
    birth until death.

Although the steps of the *sadhana* practice in the old and
    new traditions[121] are different,
They share the same aim of purifying the illusion created by
    emotions,
Just like an eye disease is cured with either a scalpel[122] or a
    surgical needle.[123]
Each illness has its own cure:
A hot disease demands a cool medicine; a cold disease,
    a hot remedy[124].
In the same way, the various courses of purification correspond
    in number to the problems to be purified.
Curing an eye disease with a scalpel or medicine
Is the same insofar as they both relieve the eye problem.
Similarly, although the steps of *sadhana* practice in the new and
    old traditions are different,
They are equal in that they both purify thoughts and emotions.

Briefly, as to the manner in which purification is effected by
    meditation:
Contemplation of essential reality[125] purifies the experience of
    the previous intermediate state of the moment of death;
All-illuminating contemplation purifies the mental body of the
    intermediate state;

Contemplation of the cause, including visualization of the
    lotus, sun, and moon seats,
Purifies the basis of the body, the white semen of the father
    and red ovum of the mother.
Visualization of the seed syllable purifies the consciousness
    that enters the womb;
Transformation of the syllable into the symbol of the deity
    and again visualization of the syllable
Purifies the embryonic process, the phases of watery, gathering,
    flesh-forming, and the other fetal stages.[126]
The complete form of the deity purifies the formation of the
    body and birth.
The consecration of the three places purifies the karmic traces
    of the three doors.
Womb birth is purified through the method of the five actual
    awakenings,[127]
And the other birth modes are purified in a similar way.[128]

Some Anuttaratantras speak of
Causal Vajradhara that purifies the luminous clarity of the
    intermediate state of death;
Resultant Vajradhara that purifies the intermediate state;[129]
Emanation of the mandala deities from the secret space
    (that is, the womb)[130]
That purifies the blending of the sperm, ovum, and wind
    energy which are the basis for the formation of the body
    of habitual tendencies;[131]
Gradual dissolution of the three letters[132] that purifies the three
    lights of appearance, increase, and attainment;[133]
And the sphere[134] that purifies the white and red light.[135]

Understanding this alone, although there are many methods,
    you can unravel it all.
Merging with the wisdom mandala[136] purifies physical trainings
    and other worldly disciplines;[137]
Initiation and sealing[138] purify the inheritance of the paternal
    lineage;[139]
Homage, confession, offerings, and praise purify the enjoyment
    of sense objects;
Recitation of the mantra purifies senseless speech.
The phases of dissolution purify the intermediate state of
    death following this life,
And reemergence in the deity's form[140] purifies the intermediate
    state.
This presentation is only a summary; I will not elaborate
    further.

The preliminary refuge and *bodhichitta* as well as the dedication
    and aspirations at the end of the *sadhana*,
Are indispensable practices in Mahayana.
The consecration of the offering, the tantric feast, and so on,[141]
Are branches that effortlessly accomplish the two
    accumulations.
The basis of purification, the essence of enlightenment itself,
Is the deity's form, clear and complete with the major and
    minor marks.
Thus, by meditating on the form of a similar deity as your
    path,
You will realize the result of purification, the dimension of the
    deity that has always been present.
At the time of the ultimate result of liberation, this is called
    the attainment of the state of Vajradhara.

Whether you meditate in an elaborate or a simplified way
  during the phase of creation,
The clarity of form purifies the clinging to all perceptual
  objects.
Recollecting the real sense of what is visualized[142] frees you
  from holding to material characteristics,
And feeling the stable pride of the deity vanquishes fixation
  on the common I.
As a result of having become somewhat familiar
With each aspect of the visualization such as the head, arms,
  and legs,
You can finally meditate vividly on the entire form.
If this meditation is not stable and thoughts stream forth,
Aim your awareness on a symbol, such as the *vajra* in the
  deity's hand.
If you are agitated, concentrate on the crossed legs.
If drowsy, direct your awareness to a detail such as a jewel on
  the deity's crown.
If the form is murky and unclear,
Even though many thoughts are not pouring forth,
Place before you a painting
With brilliant colors or a statue of good quality,
And gaze upon it for a long time and without any movement
  of thought.
Then immediately visualize your body as that image
As this will increase the quality of your meditation.

Even if you recollect the real sense of each aspect of the
  visualization,
This mental consideration will increase discursive thought

And beginners will find it a secondary cause for distraction and lack of clarity.
Therefore, meditate on the deity's form as empty and luminous like a rainbow,
Knowing that the creator of that form is your own mind,
The essence of which is from the beginning empty and without origin,
Displaying its extraordinary qualities
In the forms of faces, hands, and ornaments.

Do not meditate on pride; sever the root of grasping at an I.
When grasping at an I falls apart, wherever the mind focuses,
Its essence manifests directly.
In this way, by cultivating the creation phase with perseverance,
During meditation the power of concrete vision will weaken,
And even when you are not meditating, everything will manifest as the deity:
This is called the lesser degree of clear vision.
When illusory vision manifests as the deity and the celestial palace,
Regardless of whether you are meditating or not, this is called a middling degree of clear vision.
When, as a result of your meditation, gods of the form and formless realms
See you as the deity, this is called the great degree of clear vision,
Which in the old tradition is known as the knowledge holder of maturation.[143]

The clarity of the deity's form is the clarity of your own mind;
Dissatisfaction with lack of clarity is also your mind;

That which desires clarity and meditates is mind;
The wisdom master and the deity are mind:
The ultimate essential point of the path of the two phases
Is that everything is a manifestation of the unmodified essence of mind.
Thus, no matter how many creation phases you cultivate,
As long as you simply remain in a state of presence, undistracted,
Clarity or lack of clarity will be experienced simultaneously with emptiness.
Although the creation phase is contrived,
This artifice leads to the natural state.
Resting naturally in the unmodified condition,
Having understood clearly that illusory vision and grasping are fundamentally nonexistent,
Is the completion phase itself, the actual natural state.
The phase of creation is the provisional meaning, the phase of completion, the real meaning.

It is said that knowing the nature of the mind is the single knowledge that liberates all,
And that knowing many things without knowing the nature of mind obstructs
that single knowledge.
The exalted master, the great Nagarjuna said:
"Emptiness makes everything possible;
Without emptiness, nothing is possible."[144]
Thus it is taught that all the various names and conventional terms
Such as Mahamudra, Dzogchen, the Middle Way,[145] beyond concepts,

Ultimate, the state of the victorious ones, the primordial condition,
The perfection of wisdom, view, meditation, and conduct
Refer, in the real sense, to this one single reality which is the mind essence,
Beyond thought and ineffable, the fundamental nature of phenomena
That has no existence whatsoever.

Meditation on the nature of mind
Arises from within through the power of devotion,
And although explanations are not really necessary,
Ordinary persons, knowing nothing about the real condition of the mind and unfamiliar with it,
Might meditate in a blank state.

The illusory mind is composed of eight impure consciousnesses[146]
While the pure ground of all[147] is its essence.
The pure ground of all is indicated by the term essence, hence one speaks of mind essence.[148]
The all-knowing Rangjung[149] held that the eight consciousnesses include
The consciousnesses of the five senses, the sixth which is mental consciousness,
The emotional consciousness, and the ground of all consciousness.
Since the immediate mind[150] unleashes the other eight,
If not considered a category by itself, the consciousnesses can be counted as nine.
The appropriating consciousness[151] mentioned in the sutras,

The illusory mind, and cognitive obscuration
Are all synonyms for the ground of all consciousness.
Since the disposition of the ground of all is considered virtuous,
Its nature is the self-liberated essence of enlightenment.
As it abides as the ground of liberation, it is not that which must be removed.
Moreover, the eight types of consciousnesses, like a variegated rope
Mistaken for a snake, do not fundamentally exist
And are empty of identity though misapprehended as real.
When did this deception occur?
From beginningless time, coemergent ignorance has caused obscuration.
In fact, the essence of enlightenment
Is like the limpid clarity of a mirror,
While the ground of all consciousness, also known as cognitive obscuration
Or coemergent ignorance, is like the tarnish on the mirror's surface.
Emotional obscurations are the karmic imprints which accumulate
Upon the ground of all consciousness like a coat of rust.

The empty essence of consciousness is conceived of as the I
And its clarity is taken as the object.
Then through the immediate mind, which is the secondary cause for the meeting of the sense faculties with their objects,
The six consciousnesses are activated;

And though these appearances are nothing other than oneself,
  one falls prey to the power of dualistic vision.
For example, when you see a form,
Although there is no form other than the eye consciousness,
You mistake the clarity of consciousness for the form and
  its emptiness for the sense faculty.
With the immediate mind acting as the catalytic link,
At first an undeceptive and nonconceptual eye consciousness
  arises,
But it ceases immediately; the feeling of duality arises,
And the mental consciousness, the sixth, manifests.
The experience of the feelings of pleasure, pain, and
  indifference
Result in the perception of attachment, anger, and ignorance
  together with the emotional consciousness.
Then through acceptance and rejection, the accumulation of
  karma,
Also known as the conditioning aggregate, builds upon the
  ground of all consciousness.
When the mental consciousness, the sixth, associates with the
  immediate mind,
The consciousnesses of the five sense organs, looking outward,
  become objectified;
When the emotional consciousness associates with the
  immediate mind
And directs itself inward, karmic traces settle on the ground
  of all consciousness.
The karmic traces placed therein abide neutrally,[152]
And are exhausted only when their result has fully matured.

Karmic traces related to pure virtuous deeds[153]
Cannot be accumulated on the ground of all consciousness because,
At the time they are accumulated, the emotional mind transforms into a pure mind,
Antidote to habitual life, and the influence of this virtue settles on the wisdom mind.
The accumulation of merit done with virtuous intent
Manifests from the natural energy of the wisdom of the ground of all.
Apart from becoming a secondary cause for liberation and a cause for positive fruition,[154]
This merit can never be randomly exhausted.

The ground of all consciousness serves as the cause of outer phenomena,
Of inner sense organs, and all the consciousnesses between them.
The emotional consciousness is like clouds and the six other consciousnesses are like rain;
Karmic actions are like rivers;
The ground of all consciousness consisting of karmic traces is like the ocean;[155]
The immediate mind is the link that perpetuates the flow of habitual existence.

As soon as the immediate mind arises from the ground of all consciousness,[156]
Practitioners should remain in the state in which
The flow of that mind is discontinued.
This is called liberation in the first moment,

Or in canonical terms, recognition and leveling upon arising.[157]
Once the mental and emotional consciousnesses have arisen[158]
And you have recognized them with your awareness,
They are naturally liberated.
This is called liberation in the second or third moment.

Since thought is the energy manifestation of the mind,
It is impossible for thoughts of attachment and aversion
    not to arise;
But if your presence and awareness are steady, like water poured
    into a jar with a crack in the bottom,
You cannot accumulate karma.

The two equal halves of illusory thought and presence
Are called discriminating wisdom which itself examines the
    fixed thoughts,
Just like the moment when the chaff is engulfed by fire.
Although at first the flames and the chaff appear as two things,
Suddenly, upon ignition,
Both are referred to as fire.[159]

In brief, our present ordinary condition,
Like neutral darkness, without any awareness whatsoever,
Is the cognitive obscuration of the ground of all consciousness
And is also referred to as coemergent ignorance.
In the first moment the eye consciousness registers seeing a
    conch shell, for example,
Upon the meeting of the sense organ with its object, the
    consciousness is considered to be nonconceptual.
Then what is called feeling arises from that contact.[160]
The arising of aversion and attachment,

Such as delight in a lovely white conch shell,
Indicates the arrival of the emotional consciousness:
This is called the aggregate of ideation, and from that the aggregate of conditioning tendencies arises.[161]

In this way turns the wheel of existence with its twelve interdependent links.[162]
The eye consciousness and the mental consciousness cannot be blocked even if you try.
Although they do not have the power to accumulate karmic traces,
If thereafter you fall under the sway of the emotional consciousness,
You become like an ordinary person lacking the essential points of view, meditation, and conduct.
Thus, you accumulate karmic traces on the ground of all consciousness,
So try not to fall prey to its power.
The immediate mind which provides the link for the continuity of habitual existence
Is like the force of a river.
Thus, if you are skillful in applying the understanding of the crucial point of the eight consciousnesses as a way of practice,
By your cutting through the dualistic subject-object relation between the six consciousnesses and their objects,
The secondary cause of the six sense objects will not be able to rattle your state of contemplation.
This is the beginning of the sense consciousnesses turning inward.

At this point, visions of smoke, mirage, blazing black light,
   and so on, manifest, [163]
Signs that the ten winds[164] have become a viable means.[165]
The power of concrete vision declines, and unobstructedly
Countless forms of deities, luminous spheres and so forth,
Will appear spontaneously wherever one looks, outside, inside,
   in one's body or mind,
Without effort, hope, or fear.
As signs of gaining proficiency,[166] one is no longer fond of
   engaging in distracting behavior,
Senseless conversation, activities, or intimate relationships;
One desires to stay only in secluded places free from
   distractions;
The stream of thoughts ceases and one's state becomes like a
   cloudless sky.
In one's body and mind countless experiences of bliss, clarity,
   and nonthought arise.

However, these experiences offer only a partial understanding.
They are not at all the attainment of the levels of realization,[167]
   but simply signs of progress on the path.
In fact all the realized ones have said that whatever appears as
   an object
Has birth, abiding, and change, and cannot withstand
   scrutiny.[168]
The manifestation of self-originated wisdom, objectless and
   all-penetrating,
Is called the wisdom of realization.
At that time, the wish for view, meditation, and conduct ceases,
And you settle into the state of ordinary consciousness.[169]

Having definitively understood what you possessed from the beginning,
You are like a relaxed person who has completed his work:
This is the dropping of all effort, the ultimate result.

Albeit nonexistent, illusory vision manifests in various ways.
Though it appears, being empty, it is not real.
Mind essence, radiant natural awareness,[170] groundless and without root,
Cannot be said to be existent, nonexistent, or otherwise.

In Mahayoga[171] and the higher systems
The superior view is the indivisibility of total purity and the truth of suffering.[172]
When the ultimate is realized through meditation on the two phases,
The relative without base or source disappears in itself.
Therefore, if you understand that habitual life and freedom are just vision and mind
And do not exist as anything whatsoever, yet manifest as everything,
You have arrived at the essential point of learning and reflection.

The treasured crux of the entire application of training
Through the various methods of creation and completion with or without a supporting focus,
Such as purifying, transforming, or leaving illusory visions as they are,
Is that thoughts related to the past, present, and future,
Like ripples in water, never come to an end.

Without following them, maintain the watchman of presence
On whatever is your object of meditation,
And like an artisan spinning yarn, neither too tight nor too loose,
Know how to accord with your disposition.
When you gain a slight familiarity with meditation, your moments of presence will increase,
And experiences, such as the undivided state,[173] will gradually arise.
Do not allow the ordinary undercurrent of thoughts,
The dregs of mind or cognition, more harmful than drowsiness and agitation, to obscure awareness.
Bring forth the sharp edge of clarity!

When you investigate mind's nature thoroughly,
You will find that even though it manifests as variety, only one exists.
Such single reality is unattainable by grasping,
Unseen though looked at, with no color or shape.
These are signs of its being groundless, without root, and beyond concept.
Its empty essence, its clear nature,[174] which are the reflective and displaying modes, and its uninterrupted energy, which is the potentiality of manifestation,[175]
Are primordially perfect as the three enlightened dimensions.[176]

Even if you try, thoughts cannot be stopped,
Therefore do not block them! One comes, a second comes; let them come.
When they do come, let them go where they will and keep watch from afar.

Not having found anywhere to go, they return,
Like a crow that has glided from a ship.[177]
Then relax in this luminosity, remaining like the sea.

If you find it difficult to be in a state of undistracted presence in all circumstances,
Your familiarity with that condition is slight.
So practice maintaining continuity without feeling discouraged.

Your calm state may be stable, but if you have not freed yourself of fixing on concepts,
You will not rise above the three realms[178]
And the essence of your understanding will float away in the movement of thoughts,
Like the fractured reflection of the moon on moving water.
So first develop, as on the common path, the experience of calm abiding and then meditate on insight.[179]

The traditions of Mahamudra and those below it take mind as the path;
Common Dzogchen[180] is similar.
The uncommon *upadesha* series[181] teaches
That natural awareness itself is the path,
So that entering the practice through the path of calm abiding is not absolutely necessary.
Familiarity with naked natural awareness itself is sufficient,
Once recognized with neither exaggeration nor underestimation.
However, if that state has not been unmistakenly recognized,
The *upadesha*, although profound, will be difficult to practice.

In that case it is advisable to take the path of gradual progress.
Nonmeditation, nondistraction, leaving judgements aside,
Being with whatever arises, ordinary consciousness,
And beyond concepts, all refer to the same unmodified state.
There is no need to change the presence one has, be it the calm state or movement;
Even the idea of renewing presence and settling in contemplation is a mistake. Remaining in the state of simple natural awareness
Is what is meant by being in whatever arises, the path of all those who have gained realization.
In the system of Madhyamaka,[182] pacification and *chöd*, Mahamudra, and common Dzogchen,
The manner of integrating the practice with one's mind
Is the path of self-liberation of thoughts accomplished by looking nakedly
At whatever thought arises without doing anything about it.
On the path of the quintessential Dzogchen *upadesha*,[183]
One meets the essence of the real condition
By looking inwardly at the very nature of the subject who perceives whatever thoughts arise,
And thus illusory thoughts vanish by themselves without being fixed upon.
I have known learned and realized masters to say
That the former approach is dualistic as it focuses outward,
While the latter is beyond duality as it is directed inward.
Although this may be so,
You must gain experience with definitive understanding in the three ways in which thoughts are liberated.

According to Vimalamitra's explanation,[184]
Liberation in which there is no sequence of thoughts
Is comparable to a small child gazing in wonder inside a temple;
From the first moment, he has no judgment of good or bad.
The liberation of any thought vanishing into itself
Is comparable to a snake's knot unwinding itself in space:
As soon as it appears, it dissolves without any outside help.
The liberation of thoughts that are neither helpful nor harmful
Is comparable to a thief entering an empty house:
Whether he does so or not, there is neither loss nor gain.

If you want a summary of the essence, understand that
To let go of inner effort and relax as much as possible
In the knowledge of the crucial point of the practice,
Without falling prey to the ways of ordinary beings,
Is the sign of having gained stability.
That which is called nonmeditation is the exhaustion of all effort.
In the authentic condition you find nothing upon which to meditate, but there is something to become familiar with,
And to do that, in every aspect of behavior such as eating, sleeping,
Moving or sitting, take care not to fall prey to distraction.

When alone, relax and continue to be in the natural condition.
When in a crowd, bring forth the sharp edge of presence.
Since the essence of wakeful natural awareness does not exist as anything whatsoever,
There is nothing on which to fixate, but there is something in which to remain stable.

Since natural awareness is inseparable from emptiness, it is a little difficult to appraise; But as you become familiar with it, it will be like meeting an acquaintance.
Whatever variety of vision, sound, or thought arises,
Not even an atom exists which is not a manifestation of natural awareness.

The uncommon *upadesha* of Atiyoga teaches differentiating mind from natural awareness.
Thought cannot grasp the natural state of clear light;
Thus mind is that which is unclear and its movements difficult to sever.
Natural awareness is the pure aspect, present like a lamp,
That sees without an object of consciousness the clear light's original face.
When you recognize natural awareness as it manifests vividly without an object, for example, in a moment of fear,
That definitive knowledge is called
Liberation in the unborn natural awareness of the simultaneity of movement and emptiness.
This advice is not empty bookish talk,
But the heart blood instruction of the masters that has been orally transmitted
And never revealed to boastful violators of commitments,
For the guardians of mantra watch vigilantly!

The earlier Kagyü masters taught
You need not strive for the unmodified real condition.
It is sufficient to recollect this single point:
If you meditate on the real condition, the karma and obscurations of many aeons

Are purified, and the winds enter the central channel
	spontaneously.[185]
These and other benefits beyond words are acquired.
Knowing your own natural state is the single knowledge that
	liberates all.
When your power of mind is weak, and remaining in the state
	without any fixation is difficult,
Stabilize presence by practicing the creation phase or another
	method in accordance with your disposition.

In order to maintain the state beyond fixations, apply the
	enhancing practice of merging natural awareness with space,
Integrating with the center of the sky or the depths of the
	ocean,[186]
And in this way, refresh the presence of that state.
At that time, emptiness and natural awareness will arise without
	center or limits.

There is a risk that you may err in regard to emptiness, calm
	abiding, and the neutral state.
Firstly, with regard to emptiness,
Experience your nature free from the extremes of existence and
	nonexistence, birth and cessation, eternity and discontinuity,
Directly in your state, beyond points of reference, thoughts,
	and expressions.

With regard to calm abiding,
Remain like an ocean without waves.
Once turbulent thought has been completely pacified,
Mind will be unruffled[187] without center or limits.

The neutral state means trailing after the subtle movement of thought
Once strong presence has declined.
When wakeful natural awareness returns, you gain in hindsight a view of how your thoughts have moved.
This neutral state is similar to water that disappears as it streams through underbrush,
And is seen again only when it reemerges on the other side.
If during meditation the neutral state occurs,
Tighten your presence, referred to as bringing forth nakedness;
If total oblivion occurs, exhale the stale air,
Or surmount it with loud chanting or moving about, and so forth.

When angry thoughts arise sharply,
If you look nakedly at them and leave them alone, doing nothing,
They disappear in themselves without harm or benefit.
There is no self-originated wisdom other than that.
That which arises clearly in the unfabricated state,
Has the aspect of anger but in essence is wisdom.
The empty and nonconceptual state that remains after anger has vanished
Is already union;[188] you need not search for another radiant emptiness.
Vajrasattva and such like have the same meaning as that union.[189]
Apply the same method to the other emotions.
In the real sense, there is neither meditator nor object of meditation.

When presence alone is sufficient, you have reached the peak of
    practice.
In the ultimate sense, even presence itself does not exist:
When the basis of presence dissolves into the dimension of
    emptiness, it is called wisdom,
Just as the fire goes out when the wood is completely burned.
When illusion is extinguished, the corrective too is dropped.
This is the experiential domain of all exalted ones.

This state is neither meditation nor nonmeditation.
It is not meditation as it does not have any object of focus,
And it is not nonmeditation as one is never distracted.
Simply remain in the recognition of the nature of reality.
Since the ultimate is unfathomable and beyond concept,
There is nothing to be thought with mind.
If the close association between thoughts and their objects is
    not severed,
Even if you speak of the unmodified state, you cannot dispel
    illusion.
But severing the internal perceiver from the perceived external
    object
Is still duality, even if one calls it natural self-liberation upon
    arising.
Only when there is no corrective is it truly natural self-
    liberation upon arising.

Mind essence is the mother, vision the son,
And although vision arises from fixation just as bubbles rise
    from water,
If you know it to be the nondual manifestation of energy,
This is said to be the meeting of mother and son.

Ordinary life or the emancipated state, good or bad,
    understanding or lack of understanding,
There is nothing to accept or reject: everything is empty and
    perfect from the start.
View, meditation, and conduct are just this.
All the commitments to be kept are also just this.

For this reason, Atiyoga speaks of four commitments
In which there is nothing to preserve.
Since no limits have to be kept, the commitment of
    nothingness is maintained.
As no subject or object exists, the commitment of all-
    pervasiveness is maintained.
Since everything is perfected in the essence of the mind, the
    commitment of singleness is maintained.
Since everything, with nothing excluded, is perfect in singleness,
    the commitment of self-perfection[190] is maintained.
This is the ultimate state of the victorious ones of the three
    times.

When you awaken at dawn, do not analyze your dreams
Or do anything else that encourages a lot of thinking;
Remain in a state of presence that refreshes practice,
So that during the rest of the day, natural awareness will
    separate from the convoluted residue.

If ignorance about what to give up and what to apply,
    disrespect for the teaching,
Lack of conscientiousness, and inflated emotions are present,
Errors and wrongdoings will pelt you like hail.
These are like four gaping manholes that cause downfalls.

If you always maintain presence, awareness, and conscientiousness,
Even the emotions will transform into total wisdom;
Need it be added that everything else will become virtue?
All the essential points of application depend on presence.
Without presence, you will not remember these points of the practice,
And thus the mere fact that something could be applied will be of no use whatsoever. Therefore, govern yourself with unwavering intent.
Maintaining conscientiousness in all forms of behavior
Is the same as having the Buddha himself as your best friend.

Consecrate food and drink as nectar with *Om A Hum*,[191]
And before the meal, recite the brief or extensive form
Of the *Sutra of Remembering the Precious Jewels*,[192]
Then visualize yourself as the deity, imagining that at the crown, neck, and heart
Are, respectively, the wrathful deities, knowledge holders, and peaceful deities of the hundred families.
Meditate on the principal deity as indivisible from your root master.
Imagine that knowledge holders, *dakinis*, and so on, are present,
Burgeoning from the pores of your skin like an open sesame pod,
And in a state of presence and awareness, partake of the food without attachment.
There is no problem even though what you perceive is ordinary food and drink,
Because whatever you eat has become a sacred offering at a tantric feast.

Other practices such as *guruyoga*, training your determination to become enlightened,
Creation and completion phases, and so on, or whatever other meditation you desire,
You can receive from your master.

"That which is compounded is transitory; that which is defiled is suffering;
Freedom is peace; and all phenomena are empty"
These are the four seals of the view distinguishing the Buddha's teaching.[193]
Offering *tormas* to Jambhala,[194] a pinch of food[195] to the *yakshini* Haritaka,[196]
And water to the narrow larynx[197] and blazing mouth spirits[198]
Are the four seals distinguishing the Buddha's conduct.
The Buddha said, "If you uphold these eight seals of view and conduct,
You are a follower of the victorious ones,
Otherwise you are not their disciple."

The lord who protects Tibet is the master from Oddiyana.[199]
Remembering the story of his life and his kindness, invoke him.
The divine birthright of Tibet is the Great Compassionate One,[200]
Persist in reciting his six-syllable mantra.[201]

The profound essential points for the arising of wisdom are the following:
Since the wind energy of subject and object are naturally pure,
Inhale and hold the intermediate wind effortlessly; [202]

Since whatever manifests is the door for the arising of wisdom,
Open to the sky the great crystal *kati* channel;[203]
Since whatever manifests liberates itself in a state without fixation,
Focus on the letter *Hum*, the essence of your mind.[204]
If you possess these three essential points,
You will arrive without difficulty at the primordial kingdom.[205]

Moreover, in the morning as soon as you arise,
Clear away the stale breath[206] and combine *Hum A Om* with exhaling, pausing, and inhaling,[207] respectively.
Counting twenty-one or one hundred times or so,
Breathe this way throughout the day.
Also when going to sleep, unite the three letters with exhalation, inhalation, and pausing,
And imagine breathing during the night this way.
The 21,600 breaths[208] become mantra and
Without tribulation, the recitation of the deity's mantra is fulfilled.

The king of the teaching, the incomparable Dagpo,[209] said that,
Once you have recognized the mind essence,
No path is more profound than throughout your life always holding the air slightly in the method of calm breathing[210]
While doing profound mental recitation,[211]
And from time to time, invoking the master and merging your mind with his.

Going to sleep, draw into the center of your heart the master who is at your crown, Leaving aside all mental activity that increases thoughts;

Invoke him with devotion, and then relax in the undistracted state.
Deep sleep will gradually arise as luminosity.

Dream practice which includes recognition, change, multiplication, and purification[212]
Will be easy to train in as long as you are governed
By the consideration that all daily vision is a dream.
When you fall under the power of the daytime vision as concrete,
While you may recognize dreams at night, it will be difficult to apply them as practice.
Moreover, in order to cut through the illusions of the intermediate state,[213]
You must cut through dreams.
If you do not understand that daytime vision is like a magical creation or a dream,
Continuous illusions, one darker than the next, will arise.
In general, all practices that need getting used to,
Such as meditation on death, impermanence, love, compassion, devotion,
The creation phase, dream, illusory body,[214] and the intermediate state,
Should be incorporated daily, without fail, in the four kinds of activity.[215]
In this way, you will quickly train yourself and realize them.

I and others like myself have not remembered to apply the teaching wholeheartedly, And thus have not integrated the dharma with our minds.

However, due to the good influence of positive deeds done in previous lives,
I feel a sincere faith in the teaching of the Enlightened One.
Therefore, with just this faith and with the intention to benefit others
As the primary motivation, along with the secondary cause of the request
Of Shrimat,[216] the spiritual friend whose threefold training[217] is perfectly pure,
I wrote this text, not out of qualities I do not possess,
But as the dharmaspeak of a parrot.
By this root of virtue, may the glorious Karmapa and his lineage holders
Remain for long; and through the flourishing of their enlightened activities,
May all beings throughout space attain in a single lifetime the real state of Vajradhara.

At the request of Karma Palden, an attendant to the fourteenth Karmapa, the omniscient king of victorious ones, and a spiritual friend whose mind is dedicated to the definitive meaning, I, Karma Ngawang Yonten Gyatso, who bear only the semblance of a Buddhist monk, at the age of twenty-seven gave this advice orally to Karma Palden who transcribed it.

May it be the source of excellent benefit for the teachings and sentient beings.
In all times and all directions, may glory prevail.
May the glorious blaze of auspiciousness ornament the world.
May it be virtuous! May it be virtuous!

Advice for Lhawang Tashi

Homage
To Guru Padma I go for refuge.
May the Kagyu masters inspire and help me
To turn to the teachings, my mind filled with faith,
And to follow the path to irreversible freedom.

Atisha, Lord of Tibet, offered this advice:
"In the midst of many, watch your speech.
When you are alone, observe your thoughts."
Thus he expressed two essential points.
Since the mind is the source of faults
And the mouth the gateway through which mind manifests,
Always pay attention to both of them.

Habit-ridden life and liberation are all your own mind;
Apart from that, they don't exist at all.
Pain and pleasure, good and bad, high and low,
All are simply concepts arising in your mind.
If your mind is purified, you are a buddha,
And wherever you live is a pure land.
Whatever you do is done in the state of reality.
Whatever you perceive is the rich display of wisdom.

If your mind is not purified,
Even a buddha seems to have faults.
Even your parents cause you vexation.

Circumstances seem hostile.
Hope, fear, attraction, aversion arise endlessly.
Fruitless years pass and your human life ends.
Your friendships end in clashes.
No matter where you live, you find no happiness.
However much you own, you feel dissatisfied.
Once you have one thing, you must have another.
Although you intend to practice the teachings,
Swept away by the distractions of this life,
Your life ends just as you think, "Now I'll begin."

At first you experience genuine detachment
And feel as if you could abandon everything,
Then you become so clenched shut, you begrudge even a needle.
At first you think of nothing but your master,
Overwhelmed with respect and devotion,
But after a while you find you have doubts.
At first you exude faith and confidence,
Adding to every spiritual practice immediately another,
But as you grow older, the whole effort fades into nothing.
When you find a new friend who is congenial,
You care for his health and life more than your own,
But once the novelty's gone, you regard him with hostility.

The root of all of these problems you face
Is failure to govern your mind.
If your mind collaborates,
You need not seek a solitary place;
A mind free from concepts is the real solitude.
You need not go looking for a teacher;

Mind itself is your teacher: it is the Buddha.
You need not fear advanced practices;
Mind undistracted is the essence of practice.
You need not try to avoid distractions;
If you sustain the presence of awareness, they self-liberate.
You need not panic when an emotion surges;
Once you know its nature, it is your wisdom.

Habit-ridden life and the state of liberation do not exist
Other than in the mind this very instant,
So keep a constant watch over it.
If you are unable to govern the mind within,
You will find no end of enemies without,
But if you can conquer the anger within,
You will appease all enemies on the face of the earth.
If you never know inner contentment,
Despite all your riches, you will be a beggar.
If you are graced with detachment and free of craving,
You are always a rich man, though you own not one thing.

The joy you feel in the fulfillment of good worldly deeds,
Spiritual practices, and virtuous actions,
Brings birth in the higher realms.
But that life is impermanent, still within cyclic existence.
Look at the essence of that joy; see its empty nature.
This insight will place you on the path to freedom.

Self-centered pursuit, whether worldly or spiritual,
Is tainted and the cause of suffering and frustration.
Chasing after thoughts and tormenting emotions,
Such as anger, aversion, desire, and attachment,

Leads to your birth in the three lower realms
Where existence is swollen with unimaginable suffering.
Whatever you experience - physical pain or painful emotion,
Look directly at its nature: it vanishes into emptiness.
Wisdom is none other than this.
It is crucial to keep the movements of your mind in sight at all times
By joining it to this mind of awareness.
The essence of all practices is contained in the watching of the mind.
The bodhisattva Shantideva taught the way to do this:
"Those who wish to guard their minds are instructed
To apply all aspects of mindfulness and awareness.
Placing my hands in prayer,
I beseech you to guard your mind in that way."
This is important for you! Practice accordingly!

As all objects perceived by the six consciousnesses
Are only the magical manifestations of mind essence,
If you try to reject or engage them, you become confused,
So it is best to take the route of all as one taste.
If you are a novice practitioner you are advised
To hold the highest view while acting impeccably,
Appreciate the opportunities and rarity of human life,
Think constantly about death and impermanence
And gain conviction in the inevitable law of cause and effect.

Seeing or hearing of someone's death,
Know that as a sign of your own eventual fate.
Witnessing the transition from summer to winter,
Remember that all things eventually change.

Observing bees and the seizure of their stores of honey,
Understand the futility of wealth and possessions.
Noting a house in ruin or a deserted village,
Understand that your own home will one day be empty.
Seeing others lose their loved ones,
Think that you will be separated from those close to you.
Beholding sudden misfortune befall another,
Remember that this could happen to you as well.

View everything, yourself and all others, exactly like a dream,
Without a particle of anything real.
When you remain present in your natural condition,
Your mind unmodified by attempts to change it,
You will realize the emptiness of everything, outer and inner,
The space-like union of clarity and emptiness:
This is the ultimate *bodhichitta*.

Feel spontaneous and genuine boundless compassion
Towards all who, unaware of the nature of things,
Wander in cyclic existence enduring immeasurable suffering
    and pain:
This is the relative *bodhichitta*.

Do not cling to compassion; understand it is empty.
Compassion arises as the natural energy of emptiness.
Apply yourself to this innermost practice,
The essence of the union of sutra and mantra.

Here is the way for you to realize these teachings:
Cultivate your positive potential as much as you can.
Pray to the Three Jewels and ask for their help.

Let devotion towards your teacher penetrate your being.
Turn yourself and others away from wrongdoing.
Spur yourself to do what is wholesome.
Generate the awakened mind of the Great Way,
And always selflessly dedicate all virtue to others.
Oh monk, like a glorious new moon,
May your good mind wax and
May you become like a lord of gods.

At the request of the virtuous practitioner Dévendra
This was written by the practitioner Lodrö Thaye,
Who is an old man who only eats, shits, and sleeps.

May longevity practices and dharma practices be perfected
And may the two objectives be spontaneously attained.

Sarva siddhirastu mangalam

Bibliography

Scriptures

Candraguhyatilaka
Candraguhyatilakanāmamahātantrarāja
Zla gsang thig le zhes bya ba rgyud kyi rgyal po chen po
Dg. K. rGyud 'bum, vol. Ja, ff.247b-303a (Toh.477)

Guhyasamaja Tantra
Sarvatathāgatakāyavākcittarahasyaguhyasamājanāmamahā-kalparāja
De bzhin gshegs pa thams cad kyi sku gsung thugs kyi gsang chen gsang ba 'dus pa zhes bya ba brtag pa'i rgyal po chen po
Dg.K. rGyud 'bum, vol. Ca, ff.90a-148a (Toh. 442)

Guhyasamaja Tantra, Continuation
(Sanskrit not given in Toh.)
'Dus pa phyi ma
Dg. K. rGyud 'bum, vol. Ca, ff.148a-157b (Toh. 443)

Hevajra Tantra
Kye'i rdo rje zhes bya ba rgyud kyi rgyal po (Part I)
Dg. K. rGyud 'bum, vol. Nga, ff.1b-13b (Toh. 417)
Kye'i rdo rje mkha' 'gro ma dra ba'i sdom pa'i rgyud kyi rgyal po (Part II)
Dg. K. rGyud 'bum, vol. Nga, ff.13b-30a (Toh. 418).

Also Rumtek publications, Sikkim.
Ed. and trans., D.L. Snellgrove. *Hevajra Tantra*, Parts I and II. London: Oxford University Press, 1959.

Kalacakra Tantra
Paramādibuddhoddhṛtaśrīkālacakranāmatantrarāja
mChog gi dang po'i sangs rgyas las phyung ba rgyud kyi rgyal po dpal dus kyi 'khor lo
Dg. K. rGyud 'bum, vol. Ka, ff.22b-128b (Toh. 362)

Samputa Tantra
Saṃpuṭanāmamahātantra
Yang dag par sbyor ba zhes bya ba'i rgyud chen po
Dg. K. rGyud 'bum, vol. Ga, ff.73b-158b (Toh. 381)

Sutra of Remembering the Jewels (dkon mchog dran pa'i mdo)
Ārya Buddhānusmṛti
Sangs rgyas rjes su dran pa
Dg. K, mDo sde, vol.Ya, f.54b-55a (Toh.279)
Dharmānusmṛti
Chos rje su dran pa
Dg. K, mDo sde, vol.Ya, f.55a-55b (Toh.280)
Saṅghānusmṛti
dGge 'dun rje su dran pa
Dg. K, mDo sde, vol.Ya, f.55b (Toh.281)

Indian Treatises

Abhayākaragupta
  Awn of Esoteric Instructions: Extensive Commentary on the Samputa, King of Tantras
  Śrīsamputatantrarājaṭikāmnāyamañjarī
  Man ngag snye ma/ dPal yang dag par sbyor ba'i rgyud kyi rgyal po'i rgya cher 'grel pa man ngag gi snye ma
  Dg.T. rGyud, vol. Cha, ff.1b-316a (Toh. 1198)

Jalandhara
  Sādhana of Hevajra/ Vajra Lamp: A Brief and Correct Explanation of the Hevajra Sādhana
  Hevajrasādhanavajrapradīpanāmaṭippaṇīśuddha
  Kye rdo rje'i sgrub thabs kyi mdor bshad pa dag pa rdo rje sgron ma
  Dg.T. rGyud, vol. Nya, ff.73a-96a (Toh. 1237)

Kamalarakṣita
  Sādhana of the Black Yāmari
  Kṛṣṇayāmarisādhana
  gShin rje'i gshed nag po sgrub pa'i thabs
  Dg.T. rGyud, vol. Mi, ff. 49b-57a (Toh.1932)

Lvavapa
  Sādhana of Lord Cakrasaṁvara, Called the Precious Crown Jewel
  Bhagavacchrīcakrasamvarasādhanaratnacūḍāmaṇi
  bCom ldan 'das dpal 'khor lo bde mchog gi sgrub thabs rin po che gtsug gi norbu
  Dg.T. rGyud, vol. Wa, ff. 243b-251a (Toh.1443)

Padmavajra
  Commentary on [Buddhaguhya's] Guide to the Meaning of Tantra
  Tantrārthāvatāra
  rGyud kyi don la 'jug pa'i 'grel bshad
  Dg.T. rGyud, vol. 'I, 91b-351a (Toh. 2502)

Rāhulaguyha
  Luminous Sādhana of Hevajra
  Prakāsanamaśrīhevajrasādhana
  dPal kye rdo rje'i sgrub thabs rab tu gsal ba zhes bya ba
  Dg.T. rGyud, vol. Nya, ff.96a-126b (Toh.1238)
  TBRC W232703, vol 9, pp.193-254. Delhi: Delhi Karmapae Choedhey,
  Gyalwae Sungrab Partun Khang, 1982

Tripiṭakamāla
  Lamp of the Three Ways
  Nayatrayapradīpa
  Tshul gsum gyi sgron ma
  Dg.T. rGyud, vol. Tsu, f. 16b 3-4 (Toh. 3707)

Tibetan Works

Kongtrul Lodrö Thaye, Jamgon ('Jam mgon kong sprul blos gros mtha' yas).
  Five Great Treasuries (mdzod chen lnga):
  Treasury of Precious Key Instructions
  gDams ngag rin po che'i mdzod
  18 vols. Paro, Bhutan: Ngodrup and Sherab Drimey, 1979-1981
Treasury of Precious Treasure Teachings

Rin chen gter gyi mdzod chen po
111 vols. Paro, Bhutan: Ngodrup and Sherab Drimey, 1976-1980

Infinite Ocean of Knowledge (IOK: commentary to the Shes bya kun khyab)
Shes bya mtha' yas pa'i rgya mtsho/ Shes bya mdzod
3 books. Beijing: *Bod mi rigs dpe bskrun khang,* 1982
3 vols. Palpung Monastery: *dPal spungs thub bstan chos 'khor gling,* 1844 (woodblock print)

Treasury of Mantra of the Kagyü School
bKa' brgyud sngags mdzod
8 vols. Paro, Bhutan: Lama Ngodrup and Sherab Drimey, 1982

Treasury of Extensive Teachings
rGya chen bka' mdzod
20 vols. Paro, Bhutan: Ngodup, 1976

_____. *Commentary on (Rangjung Dorje's) Profound Inner Reality*
rNal 'byor bla na med pa'i rgyud sde rgya mtsho'i snying po bsdus pa zab mo nang gi don nyung ngu'i tshig gis rnam par 'grol ba zab don snang zab mo nang don
Rumtek, Sikkim: Dharma Chakra Centre, 1981 (woodblock print)

_____. *Disclosing the Secret of the Invincible Vajra: Phrase by Phrase Commentary on the Hevajra Tantra, Two Examinations*
dPal kye'i rdo rje'i rgyud kyi rgyal po brtag pa gnyis pa'i tshig don rnam par 'grol ba gzhom med rdo rje'i gsang ba 'byed pa
Rumtek, Sikkim: Dharma Chakra Centre, 1981, (woodblock print)

_____. *Manual for the Performance of Retreat on the Tantras of Marpa's Tradition called the Jewel Ship*

Mar lugs rgyud sde rnam kyi bsnyen pa ji ltar bya ba'i yi ge rin chen gru gzings, in *Treasury of Mantras of the Kagyü School* (bKa' brgyud sngags mdzod), vol. Om. Palpung monastery (xylography)

_____. *The Light of the Sun: Garland of Views of Esoteric Instructions*
Man ngag lta ba'i phreng ba'i tshig don gyi 'grel zin mdor bsdus pa zab don pad tshal 'byed pa'i nyi 'od
In: *Treasury of Precious Key Instructions* (gDams ngag mdzod), vol. Ka, pp.29-84.

_____. *Topical Commentary on the Hevajra Tantra*
sPyi don legs par bshad pa gsang ba bla na med pa rdo rje drva ba'i rgyan
Palpung Monastery (woodblock print)

Longchenpa (kLongchen rab 'byams pa). *The Trilogy of Finding Comfort and Ease in the Nature of Mind*
Ngal so skor gsum. 3 volumes. Gangtok, Sikkim: Dodrup Chen Rinpoche, 1973.

Longdol Lama (kLong rdol bla ma). *Sets of Terms Derived from the Awareness-Holder Collection of Secret Mantra*
gSang sngags rig pa 'dzin pa'i sde snod las byung ba'i ming gi rnam grang
Losel Literature Series, vol. 9, pp. 179-240. Mundgod, Karnataka, India: Drepung Loseling Educational Society, 1996

Vimalamitra. *Heart Essence*
Vima snying thig in: sNying thig ya bzhi. kLong chen rab 'byams (compiler). Reprint of the A 'dzom 'brug pa chos sgar edition. Darjeeling: Talung Tsetrul Pema Wangyal, 1976.

OTHER WORKS AND TRANSLATIONS

Achard, Jean-Luc. *The Three Types of Bon*. http://bonpo.wordpress.com/2009/07/26/the-three-types-of-bon/ (accessed June 10, 2012).

Chögyal Namkhai Norbu. *Birth, Life and Death according to Tibetan Medecine and the Dzogchen Teaching*. Translated by Elio Guarisco. Arcidosso: Shang Shung Edizioni, 2008.

———. *The Light of Kailash: A History of Zhang Zhung and Tibet*, vol. I: *The Early Period*. Translated by Donatella Rossi. Arcidosso: Shang Shung Publications, 2009.

———. *The Little Song for Bringing Down the Blessings of the Mahamudra*. Translated by Adriano Clemente. Arcidosso: Shang Shung Edizioni, 2004.

———. *The Precious Vase*. Translated by Adriano Clemente. Arcidosso: Shang Shung Edizioni, 2001.

Dudjom Rinpoche and Jikdrel Yeshe Dorje. *The Nyingma School of Tibetan Buddhism: Its Fundamentals and History*. Two volumes. Translated and edited by Gyurme Dorje and Matthew Kapstein. Boston: Wisdom Publications, 1991.

Gyalwa Changchub and Namkhai Nyingpo. *Lady of the Lotus-born: The Life and Enlightenment of Yeshes Tsogyal*. Translated by the Padmakara Translation Group. Boston: Shambhala, 1999.

Hakuju Ui et al., editors. *A Complete Catalogue of the Tibetan Buddhist Canons.* Sendai, Japan: Tohoku Imperial University, 1934.

Kongtrul Lodrö Thaye, Jamgön. *Rinchen Terdzo: The Great Treasury of Precious termas*, vol. one. Translated by Erik Pema Kunsang. Boudhanath: Rangjung Yeshe Publications, 1990.

_____.*The Autobiography of Jamgön Kongtrul: A Gem of Many Colors.* Translated and edited by Richard Barron. Ithaca, NY: Snow Lion Publications, 2003.

_____. **The Five Treasuries:**

The Treasury of Knowledge, Book One:Myriad Worlds: Buddhist Cosmology in Abhidharma, Kālacakra, and Dzogchen. Translated by the Kalu Rinpoché Translation Group. Ithaca, NY: Snow Lion Publications, 1995.

The Treasury of Knowledge, Books Two, Three, and Four: Buddhism's Journey to Tibet. Translated by Ngawang Zangpo, Kalu Rinpoché Tanslation Group. Ithaca, NY: Snow Lion Publcations, 2010.

The Treasury of Knowledge, Book Five: Buddhist Ethics. Translated by the Kalu Rinpoché Translation Group. Ithaca, NY: Snow Lion Publications, 2003.

The Treasury of Knowledge, Book Six, Parts One and Two: Indo-Tibetan Classical Learning and Buddhist Phenomenology. Translated by Gyurme Dorje. Ithaca, NY: Snow Lion Publications, 2012.

The Treasury of Knowledge, Book Six, Part Three: Frameworks of Buddhist Philosophy. Translated by Elizabeth Callahan, Kalu Rinpoché Translation Group. Ithaca, NY: Snow Lion Publications, 2007.

The Treasury of Knowledge, Book Six, Part Four: Systems of Buddhist Tantra: The Indestructible Way of Secret Mantra. Translated by Elio Guarisco and Ingrid McLeod, Kalu Rinpoché Translation Group. Ithaca, NY: Snow Lion Publications, 2005.

The Treasury of Knowledge, Book Eight, Part Three: The Elements of Tantric Practice. Translated by Elio Guarisco and Ingrid McLeod, Kalu Rinpoché Translation Group. Ithaca, NY: Snow Lion, 2008.

The Treasury of Knowledge, Book Eight, Part Four: Esoteric Instructions. Translated by Sarah Harding, Kalu Rinpoché Translation Group. Ithaca, NY: Snow Lion Publications, 2008.

The Treasury of Knowledge, Books Nine and Ten: Journey and Goal. Translated by Richard Barron (Chokyi Nyima), Kalu Rinpoché Translation Group. Ithaca, NY: Snow Lion Publications, 2011.

Longchenpa. *Kindly Bent to Ease Us*, vols. 1-3. Translated by H.V. Guenther. Berkeley, CA: Dharma Publishing, 1975-76.

Kunsang, Erik Pema, and Marcia Binder Schmidt. *Blazing Splendor: The Memoirs of Tulku Urgyen Rinpoche.* Hong Kong: Rangjung Yeshe Publications, 2005.

———. *The Life of Chogyur Lingpa as told by Orgyan Tobgyal Rinpoche.* Translated by Tulku Jigmey Khyentse and Erik Pema Kunsang. http://www.rangjung.com/authors/Chokgyur_Lingpa_Life.pdf (accessed June 10, 2012).

Smith, E. Gene. "Jam mgon Kong sprul and the Nonsectarian Movement" in *Among Tibetan Texts: History and Literature of the Himalayan Plateau*. Boston: Wisdom Publications, 2001.

Sodogpa Lodro Gyaltsen. *Teachings on Semde*. Arcidosso: Shang Shung Publications, Arcidosso 1998.

Tsang Nyön Heruka. *The Life of Marpa the Translator*. Translated by the Nālandā Translation Committee under the direction of Chögyam Trungpa, Rinpoche. Boston and London: Shambhala, 1995.

Tulku Thondup. *Masters of Meditation and Miracles*. Edited by Harold Talbott. Boston and London: Shambhala, 1995.

———. *The Tantric Tradition of the Nyingmapa*. Boston and London: Shambhala, 1984.

Wayman, Alex. *Yoga of the Guhyasamaja*. Delhi, 1977. Reprint, Delhi: Motilal Banarsidass,1999.

NOTES

1   Khyung or Garuda clan: one of the six original clans of Tibet. See Chögyal Namkhai Norbu, *The Light of Kailash*.

2   Milarepa (1040-1123): Marpa's main disciple and one of the yogins who founded the Kagyü school, said to have achieved complete realization in a single lifetime. His life story and songs remain to our day a profound inspiration for all spiritual seekers.

3   Kyungpo Naljor (1002-1064): disciple of the female *siddha* Niguma (Naropa's consort). He brought back to Tibet a wonderful lineage of teachings that later, known as the Shangpa Kagyü, resulted in the appearance of countless realized masters.

4   Tüsum Khyenpa (1110-1193): disciple of Gampopa and the first of an illustrious series of Karmapa incarnations. He founded the Karma Kagyü school.

5   Bön: the ancient pre-Buddhist shamanic tradition of Tibet.

6   Loden Nyingpo (1360-1385): initiated the spread of a new kind of Bön teachings in eastern Tibet and discovered the longest version of Tonpa Shenrab's biography, the famous *Dri med gzi brjid*. He, Mishig Dorje, Sangye Lingpa, and Kundrol Tragpa were known as the Four Emanation Bodies (*sprul sku rnam bzhi*) and are considered the founders of the most important lineages within the new Bön tradition. See Jean-Luc Achard, *The Three Types of Bon*.

7   Shardza Trashi Gyaltsen (1859-1933): renowned Bönpo scholar and Dzogchen teacher who best represents the Bön tradition of the nineteenth century. He wrote five large collections of works known as *The Five Treasuries* following the model of the works of Kongtrul Lodrö Thaye. Having gathered students from all traditions of Tibet, at death he attained the rainbow body.

8   Guru Padmasambhava: popularly known in Tibet as Guru Rinpoche or Precious Master. This eighth-century master from Oddiyana in western India introduced tantric Buddhism into Tibet at the time of the Tibetan king Tri Song Deutsen (790-858). His spiritual teachings inspired the foundation of the Nyingma, the earliest school of Tibetan Buddhism.

9   Derge (*sde dge*): a district in eastern Tibet, also a town, below the Drida Selmogang range (*'bri zla zal mo sgang*).

10 Shechen (*zhe chen*): an important Nyingma monastery in the district of Derge between Nangdo and Dzogchen. It was founded in 1735 by the second Shechen Rabjam, Gyurme Kunzang Namgyal.

11 Gyurme Thutob Namgyal (1787-?): a master of all five fields of knowledge; one of the teachers of Paltrul Rinpoche, Adzom Drugpa, and of the third Dodrupchen Tenpai Nyima (1865-1926).

12 *'dul ba smad lugs:* transmission of the monastic code (*'dul ba*; Skt. *vinaya*) introduced by Shantarakshita to Tibet and rekindled and spread by Lachen Gongpa Rabsal (893-?).

13 *bka' ma* and *gter ma*: orally transmitted teachings and revealed treasure teachings, respectively, of the Nyingma school. The original *bka' ma* consists of thirteen volumes codified by Terdag Lingpa in the late seventeenth century. Later, Düdjom Rinpoche expanded this collection to fifty-eight volumes which included a large number of commentaries. An even larger collection in 108 volumes has recently been prepared by Kathog monastery. The *gter ma* are numerous and are contained in various scattered collections. A larger collection that includes a large part of these treasure teachings was prepared by Kongtrul Lodrö Thaye with the help of Khyentse Wangpo in sixty-three volumes, known as *The Precious Treasury of Termas* (*rin chen gter mdzod*).

14 *dpal spung:* one of the most important Kagyü monastic centers of learning in Tibet and the residence of the successive incarnations of the Tai Situ. Palpung was built in the Derge district of eastern Tibet by Situ Chökyi Jungne in 1727.

15 Situ Pema Nyinje (1774-1853): twelfth Tai Situ and head of the Palpung monastery. He was the root teacher of the fourteenth Karmapa and Kongtrul's main Kagyü teacher. It is said that his birth was predicted by Guru Padmasambhava as his own mind emanation.

16   Wöngen Trulku, alias Karma Thegchog Tenphel: a relative of Situ Pema Nyinje.

17   *'dul ba stod lugs*: transmission of the monastic code that was introduced by the Kashmiri scholar Shakhyashri during the time of the great translator Rinchen Zangpo (958-1055) via the region of Ngari (*mnga' ris*).

18   *kong po*: a region in southern Tibet, near the border of the Arunachal Pradesh district in northeastern India.

19   Jamyang Khyentse Wangpo (1820-1892), also known as Pema Ösal Do Ngag Lingpa: an important master in nineteenth-century Tibet. Affiliated with the Sakya, he was a tertön and a Dzogchen practitioner. He was recognized by Thartse Khen Rinpoche Champa Namka Chime, a learned teacher in the Ngorpa (*ngor pa*) subschool of the Sakya. For this reason, Khyentse Rinpoche was enthroned at Dzongsar (*rdzong gsar*), a monastery of the Sakya school. His biography was written by Jamgön Kontrul Lodrö Thaye and, recently translated by Matthew Akester, is soon to appear. For a short biography see Dudjom Rinpoche and Jikdrel Yeshe Dorje, *The Nyingma School*, pp. 849-51.

20   Phapa Lha: the main disciple and successor of Nagarjuna. He propagated the Madhyamika philosophy in India and also figures among the outstanding tantric *siddhas* of India.

21   Taranatha (1575-1634): exceptional historian, prolific writer, and accomplished master of the Jonang school. He was an extremely important link in the preservation of tantric teachings and transmissions, including those brought by Marpa to Tibet, those of the completing phase of the Kalachakra tantra, and those of the Shangpa Kagyü, among countless others.

22   Terdag Lingpa aka Terchen Gyurme Dorje (1646-1714): both a disciple and a teacher of the fifth Dalai Lama. His work was essential to the transmission of the teachings of the Nyingma school. In 1676 he founded Mindroling monastery in central Tibet, which became a renowned center of learning.

23   Karmapa Tegchog Dorje (1797-1868): the fourteenth Karmapa, born in the region of Danang village of eastern Tibet. He was recognized through indications left in a letter by his predecessor, the thirteenth Karmapa. His three main teachers were Drugchen Kunzig Chökyi Nangwa, Situ Padma Nyinje, and Kongtrul Lodrö Thaye to whom he entrusted the innermost Kagyü teachings.

24   tsa 'dra rin chen brag: the Tsari-Like Jewel Rock in eastern Tibet, considered to be a power place of Chakrasamvara.

25   See note 141.

26   rdzogs chen or Atiyoga: the highest system of yoga and peak of all ways to realization, introduced to our earth by Garab Dorje, who was born in Oddiyana about three hundred years after the passing of the Buddha. According to Chögyal Namkhai Norbu, Manjushrimitra, on the basis of the three testaments of Garab Dorje, codified the Dzogchen teaching into three series: the mind series (sems sde), the space series (klong sde), and the upadesha or secret instruction series (mang ngag sde). Although the practice and teachings of Dzogchen are widespread in the Nyingma school, Dzogchen never became an institution as such, and seekers who made Dzogchen the essence of their practice have appeared in all the various Tibetan traditions.

27   Marpa Chökyi Lodrö (1012-1097): great translator and the forefather of the Kagyü tradition. An exceptional master, he visited India several times and studied with Naropa, Maitripa, Kukkuraja, and other siddhas. His efforts to learn and practice the tantric teachings were blessed by the attainment of great realization. He originated a wonderful and widespread spiritual lineage that produced as many realized beings as stars in the sky. He introduced most of the tantras of the new schools into Tibet. See Tsang Nyön Heruka, *The Life of Marpa the Translator*.

28   Chogyur Lingpa or Chogyur Dechen Lingpa (1829-1870): a treasure revealer regarded as one of the major tertöns in Tibetan history. His revealed treasures are widely practiced by both the Kagyü and the Nyingma. For his life see NSH, pp. 841-848 or *The Life of Chogyur Lingpa* by Ogyen Thobgyal Rinpoche, and also *Blazing Splendor, The Memoirs of Tulku Urgyen Rinpoche*.

29   ris med: see E. Gene Smith, "Jam mgon Kong sprul and the Nonsectarian Movement."

30   rin chen gter mdzod. See Bibliography: *Rinchen Terdzo — The Great Treasury of Precious Termas*.

31   shes bya kun khyab. Several volumes of *The Treasury of Knowledge* have been translated by the Kalu Rinpoche Translation Group. See Bibliography.

32   Vimalamitra: one of the most important Indian Dzogchen teachers and the author of the *Heart Essence* (bi ma snying thig) teachings. He also taught in Tibet where he introduced the thirteen latter tantras of Dzogchen of the mind series and Dzogchen upadesha at the time of King Trisong Deutsen. For his

life, see Bibliography: Tulku Thondup, *The Tantric Tradition of the Nyingmapa* and *Masters of Meditation and Miracles*.

33 Yeshes Tsogyal (eighth century): the principal Tibetan consort of Guru Padmasambhava and a great yogini in her own right, responsible for the concealment of many hidden teaching of the Guru. For her life, see Gyalwa Changchub and Namkhai Nyingpo. *Lady of the Lotus-born: the Life and Enlightenment of Yeshe Tsogyal*.

34 The Nyingma, the oldest tantric Buddhist tradition in Tibet, developed during the early propagation of Buddhism in Tibet. The Kadam (*bka' gdams*) and its offshoot the Gelug (*dge lugs*), the Sakya (*sa skya*), and the Kagyü (*bka' brgyud*) are the so-called new schools which originated during the second propagation of Buddhism in Tibet.

35 Kongtrul's *Five Great Treasuries (mdzod chen lnga)* 1. *The Treasury of Knowledge (shes bya kun khyab mdzod)* in three volumes, 2. *The Kagyü Treasury of Mantra (bka' brgyud sngags mdzod)* in six volumes, 3. *The Treasury of Key Instructions (gdams ngag mdzod)* in twelve volumes, 4. *The Treasury of Precious Treasure Teachings (rin chen gter mdzod)* in sixty volumes, and 5. *The Special Secret Treasury of Advice (thun mong min gsangs mdzod)* in seven volumes. See Bibliography for available translations.

36 For more information see Richard Barron's translation of *The Autobiography of Jamgön Kongtrul*.

37 *phyag rgya chen po*: the great symbol. In the sutras this expression refers to emptiness, the nature that like a seal (*phyag rgya*) marks all phenomena, and thus is great (*chen po*). In the tantras the term is used with a variety of connotations according to the specific class of tantra, but in general the great symbol (*phyag rgya chen po*) refers to the ultimate realization attained through the tantric path. Here however, Mahamudra refers to a particular system of meditation which developed in the Kagyü school from the teaching of Gampopa. Since that system resembles the four yogas of Dzogchen *semde*, it may have been derived or adapted from that, although its followers claim it originated in India.

38 Translated as *Elements of Tantric Practice*. Ithaca: Snow Lion Publications, 2008.

39 See note 172.

40 Heruka (*he ru ka*): here understood as a general name for the principal deity of the mandala, such as Chakrasamvara, Hevajra, or Guhyasamaja. See Kongtrul, *Manual for the Performance of Retreat on the Tantras of Marpa's Tradition, called The*

Jewel Ship, f.40b-3-4 in *Treasury of Mantras of the Kagyü* (*bka' brgyud sngags mdzod*), vol. Om, *Palpung* monastery, xylography.

Heruka is sometimes translated in Tibetan as *khrag 'thung*, blood drinker, a translation deemed incorrect by the scholar *Butön*, as the term refers not only to wrathful tantric deities, but also to those in a lustful mood.

41 See below, Practice of the Creation Phrase and Its Preliminaries.

42 *gtor ma*; Skt. *bali:* offering of food. In ancient India, various common foods were used for this offering. In Tibet, in what became a highly ritualized practice, the food offered was roasted barley flour (*tsam pa*) mixed with butter. The offering was molded, painted, and decorated with butter in different ways according to the particular ritual of the deity.

43 A double *vajra* (*sna tshogs rdo rje*) with empty spaces filled by smaller *vajras* is generally visualized as the ground. The enclosing fence and tent are also made of *vajras*.

44 In most cases the ten wrathful deities are imagined on the tips of the spokes. For details of the rite see Abhayakaragupta, *Awn of Esoteric Instructions: Extensive Commentary on the Saṁputa, King of Tantras* (*Śrīsaṁputatantrarājaṭikāmnāyamañjarī; Man ngag snye ma/dpal yang dag par sbyor ba'i rgyud kyi rgyal po'i rgya cher 'grel pa man ngag gi snye ma*). Dg. T. rGyud, vol. Cha, ff.1b-316a (Toh. 1198), a commentary to the *Saṁpuṭa Tantra.*

On the sphere of activity of the ten wrathful deities, see Tsongkhapa as cited in Alex Wayman, *Yoga of the Guhyasamaja*, p. 243.

45 The accumulation of merit (*bsod nams bsags pa*) is performed at the beginning of a tantric *sadhana*, though all procedures are included in the sevenfold service (*yan lag bdun pa*). Lvabapa's *Sadhana of Chakrasamvara* explains that at one's heart one imagines a letter *ram* that transforms into a sun disk. Upon that, the seed syllable of the deity radiates light of five colors. The light pervades one's body to the tip of the pores, and the pride of having transformed into the chosen deity is felt. Light emerging from the pores invites Chakrasamvara and his mandala, encircled by the eight charnel grounds, to be present in the sky before oneself. In front of the charnel ground in the east, on a throne encrusted with jewels, one's master is imagined as Chakrasamvara, seated on a blossoming golden lotus. First paying homage (*phyag 'tshal ba*) to the master, the deity, and all the buddhas, one then makes offerings to them (*mchod pa*) in order to attain awakening for the welfare of all beings. From the letter at

one's heart emanate sixteen goddesses, such as the one holding the vina who performs outer offerings. Four other goddesses, such as Matangi, holding skull-cups full of nectar, perform the inner offering. The secret offering of the real condition consists in imagining that the master enters into union with his consort and experiences the supreme delight. Having made such offerings, one confesses past mistakes (*sdig pa bshags pa*) and pledges not to repeat them in the future. Rejoicing in the virtue (*dge ba rjes su yi rangs ba*) of the buddhas, bodhisattvas, and ordinary people, one dedicates all one's virtue for the attainment of unsurpassable enlightenment (*bsngo ba*). Until that goal is accomplished one takes refuge (*skyabs su 'gro ba*) in Chakrasamvara, the union of all buddhas, in the mantras and mudras he has revealed, and in the *dakinis* of the mandala. Urging the buddhas to promulgate the teaching (*chos kyi 'khor lo bskor ba bskul ba*) so that the obscurations of all beings may be dispelled, one entreats them not to pass into perfect peace and remain present for aeons (*mya ngan las mi 'da' bar gsol ba 'debs pa*). These requests may be performed, however, in a different order. After the sevenfold service, one resolves to attain awakening for the sake of leading all beings to the same state and asks the buddhas to help settle oneself firmly on the path of Tantra, imagining empowerment by them. Thereafter the mantra of the hundred syllables of Vajrasattva is recited and the deity dissolves into the dimension in which no concept of offerings, of one who offers, or of a recipient of the offerings exists. *Sadhana of Lord Chakrasamvara, Called the Crown Jewel*, Dg.T. Rgyud 'grel, vol. Wa, ff.244a7-245b4 (Toh. 1443). Although not mentioned here, the four immeasurables of love, compassion, joy, and equanimity are also contemplated at this point as a preliminary to the main phase of every extended tantric *sadhana*.

46 The main elements of the mandala of the residence symbolize the thirty-seven factors of enlightenment (*byang chub kyi phyogs kyi chos sum cu so bdun*). Rahulaguyha states: "The four sides and the *vajra* lines symbolize the five powers (*dbang po lnga*); the four gates symbolize the four applications of mindfulness (*dran pa nye bar bzhag pa bzhi*); the four archways symbolize the four perfect abandonments (*yang dag pa'i spong ba bzhi*); the four crossbars (*stegs bu*) over the archways symbolize the four miraculous powers (*rdzu 'phrul kyi rkang pa bzhi*); the four corners of the palace and the ornamental pendants (*do shal phyed pa*) symbolize the five strengths (*stobs lnga*); the eight aspects of the noble path (*'phags lam yan lag brgyad*) are symbolized by the eight pillars; the seven aspects of enlightenment (*byang chub kyi yan lag bdun*) are symbolized by

the portals, balconies, parasols, yak tail fans, canopies, bells, and banners." *Luminous Sadhana of Hevajra*, Dg.T. Rgyud 'grel, vol. Nya f.102b4-6 (Toh. 1238).

47 Tib. *dur khrod brgyad*; Skt. *smasanartaka*: the eight charnel grounds, named in the tantras in diverse but similar ways.

48 *gnod sbyin* : one of the eight classes of gods and demons (*lha srin sde brgyad*), the *yakshas* are a large class of beings originally dwelling in trees and so forth, sometime conjured as helpers by *siddhas*.

49 *klu*: serpentine demigods who dominate the underground world and the waters. One of the eight classes of gods and demons, the *nagas* are often conjured for favors in India and the Himalayas. It is believed that a wrong contact with them or their environment can cause provocations and illnesses.

50 *mchod rten*: originally funerary monuments housing the relics of saints, they are symbolic monuments of spiritual support for the aspirations of beings.

51 According to Jalandhara, the eight charnel grounds are symbols for the purity of the eight consciousnesses: the five sense consciousnesses: (*dbang shes lnga*) plus the ground of all consciousness (*kun gzhi rnam shes*), the mental consciousness (*yid*), and the emotional consciousness (*nyon mongs kyi yid*). Moreover, they represent the purity of the eight analogies for unreality: a reflection in a mirror (*me long nang gi gzugs brnyan*), a dream (*rmi lam*), a magical creation, an optical illusion (*mig rgyu*), a city of *gandharvas* (*dri za'i grong khyer*), an echo (*brag cha*), a reflection in the water (*chu nang gi gzugs brnyan*), and space (*nam mkha'*). Dg.T, Rgyud 'grel, Vol. Nya f. 78a7-b2 (Toh. 1237). For a detailed description, see Rāhulaguhya, Dg.T, Rgyud ,grel, Vol. Nya f. 101b7-102b3 (Toh. 1238).

52 *sgrub thabs*: originally the whole range of the individual spiritual praxis. Here it refers to particular texts whose recitation is meant to guide the visualization, recitation of mantras, and so forth.

53 Wisdom mandala: a representation of the divine palace and its residing deities.

54 Sealing oneself with the lord of the family (*rgyas bdag pa*): to visualize the lord of the family to which the specific deity belongs, on the crown of the head of the main deity of the mandala as well as on those of all other deities of the mandala.

55 *bdud rtsi myong ba*. Through various visualizations, mantras, and symbolic gestures, the five nectars (*bdud rtsi lnga*), namely urine (*dri chu*), feces (*dri chen*), blood (*rak ta*), semen (*byangs sems dkar po*), and marrow (*rkang mar*); and the five types of flesh (*sha lnga*): human (*mi*), ox (*ba lang*), dog (*khyi*), horse (*rta*), and elephant (*glang po che*) are purified, transformed, and multiplied. Thereafter, the nectar is offered to oneself as chief of the mandala. For a detailed description of a rite, see Kamalarakshita's *Sadhana of the Black Yamari*, Dg.T. Rgyud 'grel, vol. Mi ff.1-8, ff.6a7b5 (Toh. 1932).

56 *dag pa dran pa*: literally, recollection of purity.

57 *zhu bde*: so called because the experience of bliss is caused by the melting of the white vital essence at the crown of the head.

58 *gnyis sbyor gyi dga' ba bzhi*: the four joys of sexual union that accompany the descent and reversal of the white vital essence from the crown of the head. See below, the section on Inner Heat.

59 *Hevajra Tantra*, f.26b7-27.

60 Vajra body: the subtle body comprised of channels (*rtsa*), wind energy (*rlung*), and vital essences (*thig le*).

61 *grub thob*: here, the accomplished tantric masters of India who were responsible for the discovery and propagation of the tantras and their transmissions.

62 *'phrul 'khor* or *'khrul 'khor*: physical exercises practiced in conjunction with breathing and concentrations, usually associated with various tantric cycles.

63 Mahamudra of empty form: expression used in the Kalachakra system to denote the emptiness endowed as the supreme of all aspects (*rnam pa thams cad kyi mchog dang ldan pa'i stong pa nyid*). According to the Kalachakra, this emptiness alone is capable of producing supreme immutable bliss (*'gyur ba med pa'i bde ba chen po*), the final attainment. Its nature is like that of images in a divination mirror and has all the aspects (*rnam pa thams cad pa*) of the three realms of existence, though it lacks any real characteristic of its own, for it is not composed of particles. Free from conceptual constructs, this emptiness is direct knowledge, the illusory manifestation of the supreme (*mchog*) wisdom of clear light. See Kongtrul's *Infinite Ocean of Knowledge*, vol. III, pp. 213-218.

64 The stages of the manifestation of the luminous nature of mind occur in different circumstances during the life of an individual and particularly at the moment of death. They also occur to yogins who apply specific techniques.

For an extensive discussion, see Kongtrul's *The Treasury of Knowledge, Book Six, Part Four: Systems of Buddhist Tantras*, pp. 252-266.

65 *lus dang rtsa'i stong ra:* literally, empty enclosure of body and channels. This means to visualize one's body in the form of the deity as well as to visualize the inner channels as completely hollow.

66 *gtum mo;* Skt. *candali.*

67 *a shad:* A-stroke or partial A. This is the form in which the fire element is imagined at the navel or below the navel in the inner heat practice. The shape, part of the Tibetan letter A, resembles a long, slender triangle with the tip pointed upward.

68 For the functions and locations of the five wind energies see Chögyal Namkhai Norbu, *Birth, Life and Death*. See also note 165.

69 *rdo rje'i bzlas pa;* Skt. *vajrajapa:* a breathing practice associated with syllables. Although there are many types of *vajra* recitation, all serve similar functions: loosening the coarser knots of the chakras; purifying the channels; bringing the winds into the central channel, and binding them to the vital essence therein. For an extensive discussion see Kongtrul's *Infinite Ocean of Knowledge*, vol. III, pp. 136-159.

70 See note 67.

71 *ril por 'dzin pa* and *rjes su zhig pa:* two ways of dissolving the perceivable universe and the visualization of the mandala. In the first, one imagines that one's body as the deity dissolves into light from the extremities to the center of the body. In the second, the universe dissolves into beings, then the beings into oneself as the deity, then oneself into light.

72 See note 112.

73 *spyod pa:* conduct that aids in the attainment of both kinds of power, common and supreme. A number of conducts are taught in various tantras. On this subject Longchenpa explains that, having stabilized one's experience to some extent, in order to enhance the results of the practice, one applies the deliberate behavior of awareness (*rig pa'i brtul zhugs*) in elaborate (*spros bcas*), unelaborate (*spros med*), and extremely unelaborate (*shin tu spros med*) ways. The elaborate approach is intended for a young person whose intelligence is not fully developed but who has considerable wealth. In an isolated place one builds a mandala, sets out offerings and adornments, and gathers yogins

and yoginis in numbers equal to the deities of the mandala. After having performed the creation of the deity and the completion phase, one enjoys all aspects of the gathering – singing and dancing, and so forth – without attachment. If carried out correctly, this practice will yield powers in six months. The unelaborate conduct is intended for persons of average wealth, intelligence, and age. It is basically the same as the above, though only a very small number of participants is assembled. The extremely unelaborate conduct is intended for someone who has little wealth, is aged, and of great intelligence. For this last form of conduct, the individual remains alone in an isolated place and engages in what is called the *kusali* conduct, being always in the dimension of emptiness and performing solely the activities of sleeping, eating, and eliminating. See Longchenpa's *The Trilogy of Finding Comfort and Ease in the Nature of Mind*, vol. Kha, ff. 35a-36b).

74 See note 15.

75 Tsokye Dorje: aka Guru Padmasambhava. See note 8.

76 *snyigs ma*: the five degenerations characteristic of the age of conflict (*rtsod dus*) we are now experiencing: lifespan, passions, beings, times, and views.

77 Profound (*zab*) refers to the completion phase; vast (*rgya*) refers to the creation phase.

78 *Vajra* brother (*rdo rje mche po*): a person with whom tantric committments are shared, in particular, as students of the same tantric master. Here it refers to Karma Palden, an attendant of the fourteenth Karmapa, cited in the colophon of this text as the person who requested Kongtrul for this advice.

79 *dal 'byor rin chen*: literally, the precious freedoms and favorable conditions of human life that enable us to pursue the way to realization.

80 *sgo gsum*: 1. the material body, like the territory of a kingdom; 2. the voice, comparable to the ministers, the aspect of energy which pervades every part of the body and serves as the base of all activities, and 3. mind, like a king who governs every action of body and voice.

81 Presence *(dran pa)*: to remember an important issue and to keep it always in mind without forgetting it no matter what the circumstances; awareness *(shes bzhin)*: precise knowledge of the positive and negative aspects of an important issue vividly present in our minds regardless of temporary factors, and independent of mental judgement. See Chögyal Namkhai Norbu, *Birth, Life and Death.*,.

82 *dkon mchog*, that is, *dkon mchog gsum:* the Three Jewels. At an outer level, these are the Buddha, his teaching, and the community of practitioners; at an inner level, the master, the meditational deity, and the *dakini*; at a secret level, the uncontrived view, meditation, and action.

83 *rtsa ba gsum*: the master, root of blessing; the meditational deity, root of attainments; and the *dakini*, root of activity.

84 Ludrup: the leading figure of the Madhyamika school of Buddhist philosophy and a tantric *siddha*. Nagarjuna was born in south India about four hundred years after the Buddha.

85 *bsags sbyang:* various practices to purify negative karma and to accumulate merit in its twofold aspect of performing good deeds and meditating to develop wisdom.

86 *gnas lugs*: the actual way in which all phenomena exist.

87 *lta ba*, *sgom pa*, and *spyod pa*: respectively, view, meditation, and conduct, the three principles included in any genuine way to realization.

88 *bcos ma:* artificial or artful; Skt. *utpatti*, creation: the creation phase of meditation that denotes creation by thoughts or contrived constructs built by thoughts. For this reason this phase is also called the phase of imagination (*brtags pa'i rim pa*) or artful yoga (*bcos ma'i rnal 'byor*).

89 *yongs grub*, perfect, or *rnal ma*, natural; Skt. *nispanna*, perfect or complete: the completion phase of meditation, a state with which one needs to become familiar but which is already perfect and for which nothing is created anew.

90 The creation and completion phases are vast (*rgya che ba*) and profound (*zab pa*), respectively, because the first phase, creation, emphasizes vision (*snang ba*), and the second phase, completion, emphasizes emptiness (*stong pa*).

91 Tripitakamala's *Lamp of the Three Ways* (*tshul gsum gyi sgron ma*) (Toh. 3707) Dg.T. rGyud, vol.Tsu, f.16b3-4), states:

Though the aim is identical, the way of mantra
Is superior by virtue of being clear (*rmongs pa med pa*),
Abundant in methods (*thabs mang ba*), devoid of hardships (*dka' ba med pa*),
And intended for persons with sharp faculties.

92 *thabs lam*: the path of method, here understood as the way of mantra in general. The following words from the *Hevajra Tantra* (Toh. 418) Dg.K, vol.

Nga, f.16a4 point to the principle of the path of method:

Those perverse acts by which
Some individuals are bound,
Others turn into means through which
They become free from the bonds of existence.

Explaining this verse in his *Disclosing the Secret of the Invincible Vajra: Phrase by Phrase Commentary to the Hevajra Tantra* (f.202b5-203a3), Kongtrul says:

In brief, the same unbearable, that is, perverse, acts by which ordinary individuals are bound, completely liberate from existence those who understand the method. That is to say, although it is through desire and attachment to material possessions or persons that all beings are bound, if one knows the instructions on how to use the very nature of desire as a means for experiential advancement, by using sexual desire as the path one can become swiftly liberated. Accompanied by the intention to free all beings from cyclic existence, one will attain the fully liberated state of a buddha.

93 *mchog dang thun mong gi dngos grub*: ordinary attainments, for example, the eight magical powers such as the swift foot (*rkang mgyogs*); the supreme attainment, equivalent to total realization.

94 Although phenomena appear, they do not have real existence. Their relative manifestation and their basic unreality are indivisible like the moon that seems to be in water, but which appears there only due to circumstances.

95 *drang ba'i lam*, the indirect path that makes use of mind's concepts and imagination; *nges pa'i lam*, the direct path that aims at the unmodified natural state of the individual through noneffort and nonaction.

96 *thams cad mkhyen pa*: an appellation for the historical Buddha Shakyamuni.

97 *bsnyen sgrub yan lag bzhi*: familiarization (*bsnyen pa*), complete familiarization (*nye ba'i bsnyen pa*), actualization (*grub pa*), and great actualization (*sgrub pa chen po*). These are the four stages of tantric practice variously defined in different tantras and applied both to the phase of creation and the phase of completion. In the phase of creation this knowledge mainly delineates the meditative steps in the visualization of the mandala with the resident deities.

98 *rten bzhengs pa*: sacred objects symbolic of the Body such as statues; of Speech such as scriptures, and of Mind such as stupas of the enlightened ones.

99   Recognition: a reference to the Mahamudra (*phyag chen*) and Ati (*rdzogs chen*) systems.

100 *mi sdug pa sgoms pa:* meditation on repulsiveness which entails dwelling on components of the human body considered unpleasant or disgusting.

101 *rten 'brel:* interdependence, here referring to the twelve links through which habitual life unfolds: conditioning aggregates, consciousness, name and form, sense fields, contact, feeling, craving, grasping, becoming, birth, old age, and death.

102 *gsang ngags;* Skt. *guhyamantra:* the way of transformation commonly known as Tantra.

103 *'od dpag med:* one of the five *dhyani* buddhas and lord of the lotus family, associated with the transformation of attachment.

104 See note 40.

105 *yi dam:* the deity or enjoyment dimension (Skt. *sambhogakaya*) manifestation taken as the main focus of one's tantric practice.

106 Gyalwa Yangönpa (1213-1287): an eminent master of the Drugpa Kagyü school. He was a student of Gyalwa Götsangpa (1189-1258), famous Drugpa Kagyü master, and Ko Dragpa Sönam Gyaltsen (1181-1261), who did not belong to a particular school.

107 *rdo rje 'chang:* holder of the knowledge of the indestructible state: the primordial buddha in the new schools and a symbol of the knowledge of one's primordial condition and tantric goal.

108 Heruka Chakrasamvara: a major meditational deity belonging to the Anuttara mother tantras.

109 *sor rtog ye shes:* one of the five wisdoms, characterized by the pure nature of attachment.

110 *chos dbyings;* Skt. *dharmadhatu.* The expanse of the true nature of reality, the empty nature and source of everything.

111 *bde gzhegs snying po;* Skt. *sugatagarbha:* essence of enlightenment that resides in every sentient being as inherent as oil is in the sesame seed. Here it is equated with the ultimate dimension of phenomena.

112 The final result of enlightenment is posited as the three dimensions (Tib. *sku;* Skt. *kaya*). These are the emanated dimension (*sprul sku; nirmanakaya*) vis-

ible to those who have pure perception, the enjoyment dimension (*longs sku; sambhogakaya*), accessible to bodhisattvas on the higher levels of realization (together called the form dimensions (*gzugs sku; rupakaya*), and the reality dimension (*chos sku; dharmakaya*), which has a double aspect as the wisdom dimension (*ye shes chos sku; jnanakaya*) and the essential dimension (*ngo bo nyid sku; svabhavikakaya*).

113   *mtshan dpe*: signs, such as the sixty qualities of speech that specifically characterize the emanated dimension. In stating that the essence of enlightenment possesses the major and minor marks, Kongtrul shows his adherence to Jonang Taranatha's view that the essence of enlightenment possesses all the signs and marks of the emanated dimension, a point of view upon which the other schools of Tibetan Buddhism do not agree.

114   *snyoms 'jug gi sgrib pa*: an impediment that obstructs the even state of meditative absorption. Emotional obscurations (*nyong rmongs pa'i sgrib pa*) include grasping at reality and the resulting emotions such as attachment and anger which hinder the attainment of liberation. Cognitive obscurations (*shes bya'i sgrib pa*) that hinder full realization are the concepts of subject, object, and action.

115   *dbyibs kyi rnal 'byor*: one of three yogas including shape, mantra, and reality, which are also the means of expounding the *Mahamaya Tantra* in the new schools. The essential nature of shape denotes the phase of creation and reveals the body itself as the emanated dimension of awakening. See Kongtrul, *The Treasury of Knowledge: Systems of Buddhist Tantras*, the section on *Special Methods in the Yogini Tantras*.

116   Five actual awakenings; *mngon byang lnga*: in the phase of creation of the Anuttaratantras, five successive steps in the process of generating the deity, corresponding to the five wisdoms, explained in the tantras with slight differences. For instance the *Hevajra Tantra* (Toh. 417) Dg.K, vol.Nga, f.9a2-3, explains them as follows:

The moon is mirror-like wisdom,
The sun, the wisdom of sameness,
The symbol marked by the seed syllable of one's deity.
Is called discriminating wisdom.
The merging of all into one is the wisdom of activity,
The full manifestation of the deity is the wisdom of the ultimate dimension.

The wise should meditate on these five aspects
As explained in the rite.

Thus, visualization of a moon disk is the first awakening; the sun disk, the second; the symbol, the third; the merging of these into one, the fourth; and the manifestation of the body of the deity, the fifth.

117 *rdo rje bzhi*. In this procedure, first one meditates on emptiness, and thereafter on a lotus, sun, and other seats, imagining a moon, sun, and seed letter that radiates light. Reabsorbing light, the deity manifests completely. Lastly, the three letters are visualized at the three places, head, throat, and heart, and at the sense organs. These four *vajras* are taught in the *Continuation of the Guhyasamaja Tantra* (Toh. 443) (Dg.K, vol. Ca, f.154a4-5).

First is awakening through emptiness,
Second is transformation into the seed letter,
Third is the full manifestation of the divine body,
And fourth is the placement of the letters.
Through these four *vajras*, one should
Perform the ordinary familiarization practice.

118 *cho ga gsum*. In this procedure, on a seat of lotus, sun, and so on, one imagines the seed letter of the deity that transforms into a symbol marked by the same letter which then fully manifests as the divine body as described in the *Hevajra* and other tantras.

119 *brdzus skye:* miraculous birth, the fourth type of birth, by which gods and hell beings are born.
  Explaining the four types of birth, in his *Topical Commentary on the Hevajra Tantra*, Kongtrul states that (63a2-6): "Womb birth (*mngal skyes*) is the exit from the womb after one has been conceived through uniting the father's semen and the mother's ovum. Such birth has features corresponding to the visualization of the deities emanated from the seminal essence of the male and female deities in union. Birth from eggs (*sgon skyes*) results in a form of life that is generated from the mixing of consciousness with the red and white vital essences of animals. This type of birth has features corresponding to the arising of the deity from the merging of the sun, moon, and symbol into a sphere of light. Moreover, the creation of the deity through the five steps of actual awakening following the melodious words of request from four female deities of the mandala corresponds to womb birth, while the generation of the deity through the five steps of actual awakenings with-

out songs of invocation corresponds to egg birth. Birth from warmth and moisture (*drod gsher skyes*) is a result of consciousness entering the union of warmth and moisture. This type of birth has features corresponding to the deity arising simply from a seed syllable upon a moon base. Instantaneous or miraculous birth (*brdzus skyes*) is the emergence of life instantly without any causal substance. This is similar to the deity created instantly from luminous clarity without even the seed syllable as a support."

In his *Manual for the Performance of Retreat on the Tantras of Marpa's Tradition*, called *The Jewel Ship* (f.12a4-7) Kongtrul says:

"All the above creations applied in one *sadhana* are explained as follows: the deities of the consecration of the eye, and so forth, correspond to miraculous birth. Creation through the five actual awakenings corresponds to birth from heat and moisture. The retinue deities projected outside the womb of the consort correspond to womb birth. Manifestation from a round sphere corresponds to birth from eggs."

120 A short discussion on this topic appears in Kongtrul's *Sheja Kunkhyab*, vol. III, pp. 169-170.

121 *gsar ma:* the new tradition of the tenth and eleventh centuries, originating with the translations of the tantras in the time of the famed Rinchen Zangpo (965-1055). The old (*rnying ma*) tradition originated with the earlier translations of the tantras (eighth century).

122 *gtsag bu:* a scalpel-like class of surgical instruments in Tibetan medicine generally used for extracting impure blood. It can be of six different kinds, such as an ax-headed implement, used in cases of redness of the eyes, migraine, depression, colics, menstrual disorders, and so on.

123 *thur ma*: a needle-like class of surgical instruments used in traditional Tibetan medicine to remove cataracts, pericardial effusion, and other diseases.

124 According to the principles of traditional Tibetan medicine, disorders can be classified in two general categories, hot (*tsha ba'i nad*) and cold (*grang ba'i nad*). Hot disorders are treated with medicines that have a cool nature (*bsil sman*) and other cool methods, while cold disorders are treated with medicines that have a warm nature (*drod sman*) and other warm methods.

125 Contemplation of essential reality (*de bshin nyid kyi ting nge 'dzin*), all-illuminating contemplation (*kun tu snang ba'i ting nge 'dzin*), and contemplation of the cause (*rgyud ting nge 'dzin*) are the three steps in the creation of the deity according to the inner tantra of Mahayoga of the old or Nyingma tradition.

In *The Light of the Sun,* Kongtrul comments (p. 311, 3):

"Contemplation of essential reality means abiding in a state of equanimous contemplation free of concepts, all-pervading as space. All-illuminating contemplation corresponds to the arising of impartial compassion, even though it is like a magical illusion, toward all beings that do not understand the essential nature. Contemplation of the cause, which depends on the two preceding ones, consists in visualizing a syllable, for example the letter *Hum,* as the essence of the wisdom of the state of natural awareness, like a fish leaping out of clear water."

These three contemplations of the old school correspond to the creation phase of the new school in which death, the intermediate state, and rebirth are used as the path. The contemplation of the essential nature corresponds to the recognition of the clear light of death as the reality dimension of awakening (Skt. *dharmakaya*); the contemplation of total vision corresponds to recognizing the intermediate state as the enjoyment dimension of awakening (Skt. *sambhogakaya*), and the contemplation of the cause corresponds to recognizing the moment of birth as the emanated dimension of awakening (Skt. *nirmanakaya*).

126   *mngal gyi gnas skabs lnga:* five states of the womb, including watery (*mer mer po*); gathering (*ltar ltar po*); flesh-forming (*gor gor po*); acquiring solidity (*mkhrang 'gyur*), and moving arms and legs (*rkang lag 'gyus*). *Mer mer po* is the stage in which the embryo's outer layer is the consistency of jelly and its inner content liquid. At the *ltar ltar po* stage, the embryo outside and inside resembles curd. At the *gor gor po* stage, the embryo becomes tender flesh unable to withstand pressure. At the *mkhrang 'gyur* stage, the embryo hardens and becomes like flesh, able to withstand pressure. Then at the *rkang lag 'gyus* stage, the fetus starts to move its limbs. Terms for the initial stages of fetal development are not uniform in the tantras and sutras.

127   In this context Kongtrul describes the contemplation of the cause as the five actual awakenings.

128   This may mean that other types of birth such as birth from an egg, and so on, are also purified through the five awakenings. However some scholars assert that each type of birth requires its own specific means of purification. See note 119.

129   In the process of creation of the deity, some tantras speak of causal Vajradhara (*rgyu rdo rje 'dzin pa*) and fruitional Vajradhara (*'bras bu rdo rje 'dzin pa*), defining them in different ways. But generally the causal Vajradhara is the

chief deity created at the beginning of the *sadhana* through the five awakenings. The fruitional Vajradhara is the chief deity created after the causal Vajradhara has dissolved into semen or luminous clarity. He then reemerges as the fruitional Vajradhara upon the request of the four female deities of the mandala. These female deities symbolize the four immeasurables (*tshad med bzhi*) of compassion, love, joy, and equanimity.

130   *mkha' gsang*. The most elaborate tantras describe how the deities of the mandala are first generated in the consort's womb and thereafter are propelled outward and seated upon their thrones in the mandala.

131   sperm, ovum, and wind (*khu, rdul, rlung*): the three elements whose coming together with the consciousness of the intermediate being allow the formation of a body in the womb.

132   gradual dissolution of the three letters: the dissolution of *Om Ah Hum*. In some tantras this dissolution symbolizes the consciousness of the being in the intermediate state. These letters enter the main deity, attracted by the bliss of the union of the main male and female deities. In the Hevajra *sadhanas*, after having visualized oneself as the causal Vajradhara through the five awakenings and then having dissolved into seminal essence, one becomes the fruitional Vajradhara through the three steps of creation. Once one has visualized oneself as the causal Hevajra, three letters (*Om Ah Hum*) or another symbol for the consciousness of the intermediate being, enter the mouth of Hevajra through the power of the passionate union of the lord and his consort. From the *vajra* of the father, the letters enter the lotus of the mother. As a result, Hevajra and his consort become the seminal form of molten vital essence or seed of the *vajra* mind. At this point, Pukkasi and the other three yoginis from the intermediate directions of the mandala, invoke Hevajra and his consort, urging them to manifest again in the form of the union of the father and mother. The Lord in the form of molten vital essence recollects his vow to help others and manifests again. From the sounds *Am Hum* appear a curved knife and a nine-pronged *vajra*. Lights radiate and reconverge in these two symbols that then manifest as the fruitional Hevajra and consort. Kongtrul, *Phrase by Phrase Commentary to the Hevajra Tantra* (266b7- 271a1).

133   Three lights: light (*snang ba*), the spread of light (*snang ba mched pa*), and the culmination of light (*snang ba thob pa*). These three lights which occur upon the dissolution of the elements at the end of the death process, mark the stages immediately preceding the manifestation of the clear light (*'od gsal*) of death.

134 *thig le:* the sphere of vital essence, here possibly referring to the sphere of vital essence into which the main female and male deities dissolve before reemerging as the resultant Vajradhara.

135 *snang ba dkar dmar:* a reference to the white light (*snang ba dkar lam pa*) that is experienced at the time of death as the white vital essence obtained from the father which descends from the crown of the head to the heart; and to the red light (*nang ba dmar lam pa*) that is experienced at the time of death as the red vital essence obtained from the mother which ascends from the navel to the heart.

136 Wisdom mandala: the mandala of the deities that have always existed and that are invited from the dimension of space. These deities are known as wisdom beings (*ye shes sems dpa'*; Skt. *jnanasattva*) and merge with the mandala and the deities that one has generated as the pledge beings (*dam tshig sems dpa'*; Skt. *samayasattva*).

137 '*khrul spyod*, emended to *phrul spyod*.

138 "Initiation" is described as follows: "To receive initiation, one imagines that light radiating from the seed letter at one's heart invites the initiating deities. One makes offerings, entreating them, and thereafter these deities bestow the initiation. In most tantric texts the initiation is conferred by deities that are identical to the mandala figures that one has meditated upon. As to the initiation that is conferred here, the majority of tantric works mention only the water initiation. Saroruha and Atisa, however, describe the bestowing of four initiations." See Kongtrul, *The Treasury of Knowledge, Book Eight, Part Three: The Elements of Tantric Practice*8, p. 97.

"Sealing" refers to visualizing the lord of the family on the crown of one's head and also on those of the other deities of the mandala.

139 *pha skal phog:* as in the Indo-Tibetan custom, possibly signifying acquisition of the paternal lineage at birth.

140 Reemergence in the deity's form: reemergence of oneself in a simple form of the deity at the conclusion of the *sadhana* after the mandala has been dissolved.

141 "Consecration of the offering": various offerings are consecrated in different ways. The outer offerings consist of the sense objects and the inner offerings of the five types of flesh and the five nectars. Their consecration involves dissolving and purifying them in the state of emptiness and recreating them as inexhaustible nectar through the various steps of visualization.

"Tantric feast": (*tshogs kyi'khor lo*; Skt. *ganachakra*): in the tantric praxis, mainly a method to enhance the result of one's practice. Ideally, the mandala is recreated in a house built to certain specifications; with yogins and yoginis matching the number of the deities in the mandala, food, drink, music, songs, and sexual union are enjoyed in a nondual state.

142   Kongtrul, in his *Sheja Kunkhyab*, explains that when wearied of visualizing the deity, one can recollect the two types of purity (*dag pa dran pa*). Regarding the purity of the deity, one recollects that the aspects of the visualization of a deity's eyes, limbs, ornaments, and so on, are in a real sense the supreme qualities of the enlightened ones. Also it can be recalled that one's aggregates, elements, and vital essences, and so on, are deities.

As for the ultimate purity, one recalls the purity of the nature of things, the emptiness or the unborn nature of all phenomena, remembering the purity of innate nondual awareness in which one recognizes that all phenomena are the play of innate bliss and emptiness. Masters have explained that the purpose of recollecting the real meaning of what is visualized is to overcome the concept that the path and result are different.

143   *rig 'dzin*; Skt. *vidhyadhara*. From a general tantric perspective, awareness (Tib. *rig pa*; Skt. *vidhya*) denotes the wisdom of immutable supreme bliss which is primordially present as the ground, or nature, of being. To become a holder (Tib. *'dzin pa*; Skt. *dhara*) means to reawaken such pristine awareness (in the sense of becoming aware of it again) by means of special tantric techniques. See *The Trilogy of Finding Comfort and Ease in the Nature of Mind*, vol. Ka, ff. 174a3-175b6.

The Nyingma school classifies awareness holders into four groups, namely: the awareness holder of maturation (*rnam par smin pa'i rig 'dzin*), the awareness-holder with the power over the lifespan (*tshe la dbang ba'i rig 'dzin*), the awareness holder of the great symbol (*phyag rgya chen po'i rig 'dzin*), and the self-perfected awareness holder (*lhun gyis grub pa'i rig 'dzin*). Longchenpa in his *Finding Comfort and Ease in the Nature of Mind* explains that the first awareness holder refers to practitioners of the phase of generation and the phase of completion who abide on either the path of accumulation or the path of preparation. Although such practitioners still have ordinary bodies, they have actualized their mind as the body of the deity. If such practitioners die before having achieved the supreme state (*chos mchog*) of the path of preparation, they will realize, discarding their body and with their mind ripening into the form of the deity, the great sea in the intermediate state.

The second type of awareness holder refers to practitioners who have attained the supreme state of the path of preparation and the resulting indestructible body beyond death and birth, and thus have control over their lifespan. The mind in this case turns into the mind of the path of seeing.

The third type of awareness holder refers to practitioners who abide on the first to the ninth levels of awakening. Here the body manifests as the mandala of the deity. The mind is the wisdom devoid of adherence to conceptual limitations according to the process of overcoming the obscuration found at the respective levels.

The ultimate awareness holder refers to practitioners who have attained the fully awakened state. See *The Great Chariot*, in the *Trilogy of Finding Comfort and Ease in the Nature of Mind*, vol. Ka, ff. 174a3-175b6.

144   Since emptiness is the lack of the true existence of phenomena, its very nature makes the existence of all phenomena possible.

145   Middle Way (*dbu ma*; Skt. *madhyamika*): the system of Buddhist philosophy that, along with the Mind Only system (*sems tsam*; Skt. *cittamatra*), forms the theoretical basis for the Mahayana path. The central assertion of the Madhyamika is that all things, persons, and other phenomena are devoid of an identity and only exist as mere mind attributions.

146   *rnam shes tshogs brgyad:* the eight groups of consciousness described, in the context of the Mahayana, by centrists (Madhyamikans) and idealists (Cittamatrans). These are: the ground of all consciousness (*kun gzhi rnam shes*); emotional consciousness (*nyon yid rnam shes*); mental consciousness (*yid kyi rnam shes*); and the five sense consciousnesses (*sgo lnga'i rnam shes*). The ground of all consciousness is described as a neutral mind which serves as the ground for the accumulation of seeds or predispositions for the arising of the elements, aggregates, and sensory fields of sentient beings. This consciousness knows only the facticity of objects but not their details. It is called the ground of all or basis for everything because it serves as the foundation of cyclic existence (Skt. *samsara*) and freedom (Skt. *nirvana*). After diamond-like contemplation has arisen, this consciousness transforms into the mirror-like wisdom. The emotional consciousness arises in the aspect of a self-admiring mental state, derived from the pride associated with thinking in terms of an I. It is neutral but obscured by afflictions and serves as the main condition for the arising of mental involvement. Upon the attainment of awakening, it transforms into the wisdom of equality. The five sense consciousnesses perceive the details of objects by clearly focusing upon them. They are neutral but arise

as virtue or nonvirtue due to the types of mental factors accompanying them. The mental consciousness which perceives mental phenomena upon the attainment of awakening transforms into discriminating wisdom, and the five sense consciousnesses transform into the accomplishing wisdom. See *Sheja Kunkhyab*, vol. II, pp. 386-397.

Padmavajra explains mirror-like wisdom (*me long lta bu'i ye shes*) as the realization that appearances are without identity. Wisdom of total sameness (*mnyam nyid ye shes*) is the realization that does not discriminate between oneself and the other. Discerning wisdom (*sor rtog ye shes*) is the realization that the general and specific characteristics of phenomena are without identity. Accomplishing wisdom (*bya ba grub pa'i ye shes*) is working for the welfare of oneself and others without partiality. Wisdom of the ultimate dimension of phenomena (*chos dbyings ye shes*; Skt. *dharmadhatu jnana*) is the nature of the other four as well as their objects. See Padmavajra, *Commentary on (Buddhaguhya's) Guide to the Meaning of Tantra*, Dg.T, vol. I, f. 98a4-5 (Toh. 2502).

147   Ground of all (*kun gzhi*): the essence of enlightenment, the very pure nature of the mind of all sentient beings. It is called ground of all because when it is not recognized, it serves as the cause for the deceptive visions of habitual life; when it is recognized, it serves as the cause for the pure vision of freedom.

148   *nyid* (itself) in *sems nyid*: rendered here as essence.

149   Rangjung Dorje (1284-1339): the third Karmapa, one of the most influential masters in the Karmapa lineage and an authority on the view of Tantra in the Kagyü school.

150   *de ma thag pa'i yig*. The immediate mind is understood in general Buddhist philosophy as the immediately preceeding moment of consciousness. It is one of the four conditions for the arising of perceptual consciousness.

151   *len pa'i rnam par shes pa*: appropriating consciousness. This is the consciousness which after death and the intermediate state assumes (*len pa*) the aggregates of a new life.

152   *lung du ma bstan pa*: having neither a virtuous nor nonvirtuous nature.

153   *rnam dkar dge ba*: pure virtuous deeds which do not result in conditioned existence but become the cause for enlightenment. These include listening, reflecting upon and applying the spiritual teachings.

154   *rnam smin*: a particular type of birth or existence.

155   Here a distinction is made between the ground of all consciousness which is the fruition of a previous life and the source of phenomena and the ground of all consciousness which is amassed by karmic traces in this life.

156   The arising of the immediate mind indicates the initial arising of the dualistic mind-movement or thought.

157   *'bur 'joms mgo thug*.

158   This refers to the mental consciousness which judges thoughts and phenomena and the consciousness of emotions which is an emotional response to that judgement.

159   Although the observer of thoughts and the thoughts which are observed appear to be different, they ultimately merge into a single unity of undifferentiated thought and natural awareness.

160   *reg pa*: the ever present mental factor that occurs upon the meeting of object, sense faculty and consciousness.

161   Here the emotional response to perception is identified with ideation (*'du shes*) From that response, the aggregate of conditioning tendencies (*'du byed*) which are the traces of past actions comes into being.

162   *rten 'brel bcu gnyis*: twelve interdependent links. See note 101.

163   Ten signs (*rtags bcu*): smoke (*du ba*), a mirage (*smig rgyu*), fireflies (*mkha'i snang*), a lamp (*sgron me*), a flame (*'bar ba*) or a blazing yellow light, a moon (*zla ba*) or blazing white light, sun (*nyi ma*) or blazing red light, *rahu* (*sgra gcan*) or blazing black light, the supreme *kala* (*cha*) or lightning (*klog*), and a great sphere (*thig le chen po*) in the shape of an azure moon globe. In the sixfold yoga (*sadanga yoga*) of the *Kalachakra Tantra*, these signs are specifically related to the yoga of the day and the yoga of the night.

164   *rlung bcu*: generally divided into five root and five branch winds. The five root wind energies are the life-sustaining (*srog 'dzin*; Skt. *prana*), downward-clearing (*thur du sel ba*; *apana*), fire-accompanying (*me dang mnyam du gnas pa*; *samana*), upward-moving (*gyen du rgyu ba*; *udana*), and pervading (*khyab byed*; *vyana*). The life-sustaining wind is the source of all ten winds, based in the central channel and present in all parts of the body. During one's life, this wind generates the idea of self and all conceptual constructs. It is also known as the emotional consciousness. The downward-clearing wind dwells below the navel where the three main channels meet, and flows downward. Its function

is to regulate the voiding or withholding of refined and residual constituents such as feces, urine, semen, and blood. The fire-accompanying wind arises from the channel called the chariot constellation at the heart and is connected to the stomach. Its function is to digest food and drink, separate the refined elements from the residual, convey refined nutrients throughout all the channels and thereby nourish and strengthen the organism, and rid it of impurities. The upward-moving wind arises from the elephant's tongue channel at the heart. It presides over the functions of the throat, swallowing food and drink, the movements of the arms and legs such as walking and the activities of speech and singing. The pervading wind flows through the pale yellow channel connected to the *rasana*, one of the three main channels of the subtle body. It dwells in all joints and allows for movements such as stretching and contracting. For a detailed discussion of these winds, see Kongtrul, *Commentary on (Rangjung Dorje's) Profound Inner Reality*, ff. 68b6–70a5.

The five branch winds include the serpent wind, turtle wind, lizard wind, gift-of-the-gods wind, and the victorious-in-wealth wind. These are also known by the alternative names of moving (*rgyu ba*), moving thoroughly (*rnam par rgyu ba*), moving perfectly (*yang dag rgyu ba*), moving strongly (*rab tu rgyu ba*), and moving resolutely (*nges par rgyu ba*); they are also known as the winds of the five goddesses (*lha mo lnga'i rlung*) or winds of the five faculties (*dbang po lnga'i rlung*). They serve as the mounts for the five sense consciousnesses. (Longdol Lama, *Sets of Terms Derived from the Awareness-Holder Collection of Secret Mantra*, p. 234).

165 *las su rung ba:* viable. Once progress has been made to this point, the winds can serve to further and enhance one's practice and realization.

166 *drod rtags:* "signs of heat" indicating that one has acquired familiarity with the practice. They are the same as *nyams rtags*, signs of meditative experiences. These can present themselves in many ways, positive, negative, or coarse experiences related to the condition of the five elements, earth, water, fire, wind, and space, of one's body.

167 *sa*; Skt. *bhumi*: the ten levels of realization of a bodhisattva beginning with the joyful. These are divisions or distinctions made in terms of the obscurations that have been removed and of the wisdom qualities that have been acquired. Additional levels are described in the tantras.

168 This means that the experiences of bliss, clarity, and nonthought are not to be treated as objective reality.

169   *tha mal pa'i shes pa:* ordinary consciousness. In the Kagyü view this is the inseparability of the wisdom basis of all (*kun gzhi ye shes*) which is the root of all wisdom, and the consciousness basis of all which is the root of all consciousnesses. From the perspective of its function as the basis for enlightenment, ordinary consciousness is termed the essence of enlightenment. Innate bliss is the very nature of ordinary consciousness, but remains hidden until discovered through the powerful experiences induced by tantric meditations.

170   Tib. *rig pa*; Skt. *vidya*: the state of being in the knowledge of one's own primordial condition or bodhichitta.

171   See Introduction.

172   "Indivisibility of total purity and the truth of suffering": inseparability of the two truths (*bden gnyis dyer med*), the absolute and the relative. This is explained in the following way by Kongtrul:

"The superior ultimate truth is posited as the ineffable state of total presence, spontaneously perfect as the essential cause of manifestation. The creative energy of that presence—the myriad of thoughts—which manifests in and of itself as the mandala of awakened dimensions and wisdom is posited as the superior relative truth. Neither one of these two truths represents solely the side of appearance or the side of emptiness because they manifest as a total sameness, in essence indivisible. Although the two truths are designated as indivisible, this indivisibilty is not within the range of experience of ordinary beings because it transcends the objects of thoughts and expressions that try to capture it. The description superior is applied because the manner of realizing the two truths far surpasses that of the way of characteristics." *The Treasury of Knowledge: Systems of Buddhist Tantras*, ch. 18.

173   *rtse gcig:* literally, one-pointedness. This is the first of the four stages or yogas of Mahamudra (*rnal 'byor bzhi*). The other three are: beyond concepts (*spros bral*), one flavor (*ro gcig*), and nonmeditation (*sgom med*). To remain at ease and effortless in the natural and unmodified condition with a vivid presence of the six consciousnesses is undivided yoga. To rest freely, unchanging, and all pervading in the knowledge of one's state without depending on mind's creations is the yoga free of concepts. The impartial and uncategorized view free from the concepts of good and bad (which pervades the total sameness of habitual life and freedom) is the yoga of one flavor. Not to conceive anything as an object of meditation and freeing oneself even of the subject that meditates and thus to pass into the inconceivable exhaustion of phenomena

is the yoga of nonmeditation. See Chögyal Namkhai Norbu, *The Little Song for Bringing Down the Blessings of the Mahamudra*, translated by Adriano Clemente.

174 "In the Dzogchen teaching, essence, (*ngo bo*), nature (*rang bzhin*), and potentiality of manifestation (*thugs rje*) are known as the three primordial wisdoms (*ye shes gsum*). Essence is the wisdom of primordial purity (*ka dag*), nature is the wisdom of self-perfection (*lhun grub*), and the potentiality of manifestation is the wisdom of uninterrupted manifestation. These wisdoms are present as one's primordial potential and they become manifest as the three dimensions of awakening - reality, enjoyment, and emanated dimensions of awakening - when one fully realizes one's own primordial state. However, these three wisdoms are reflected in the condition of one's mind: the essence, primordial purity, is indicated by the state of emptiness when one is in a calm state devoid of dualistic thoughts; the nature, self perfection, is indicated by the movements of thoughts, and the potentiality of manifestation is indicated by the natural awareness that one must discover within both the calm state and movement." Chögyal Namkhai Norbu, oral teachings.

175 Primary (*gdangs*), reflecting (*rol pa*), and displaying (*rtsal*) are the three modes of the potentiality of manifestation (*thugs rje*) spoken of in the Dzogchen system.

176 The empty essence (*ngo bo stong pa*) of the mind is the reality dimension (*dharmakaya*); its clear nature (*rang bzhin gsal ba*) is the enjoyment dimension (*sambhogakaya*), and the reflective and displaying mode of its potentiality of manifestation (*thugs rje'i rol pa rtsal*) that arise without interruption is the emanated dimension (*nirmanakaya*).

177 In ancient times a crow was kept on ocean-going ships in order to check the proximity of mountains or land. When the ship was in port, the crow was tied or caged, but when the ship sailed the ocean, the crow was freed. Far out at sea, in whatever direction it flew, it never found a place to land, and thus would return to the ship. See Sogdogpa Lodro Gyaltsen, *Teachings on Semde*. Arcidosso: Shang Shung Edizioni, 1998.

178 *khams gsum*: the three realms of existence, consisting of the desire realm (*'dod pa'i khams*), the form realm (*gzugs khams*), and the formless realm (*gzugs med khams*).

179 Calm abiding (*zhi gnas*) and insight (*lhag mthong*): the two main aspects of meditative practice in Buddhism, taught according to the various systems of

Sutra and Tantra. Calm abiding refers to the meditative practice of calming the mind in order to be free of the disturbance of thoughts. Insight refers to the meditative practice for discovering and being in the nature of reality.

180 With the term common Dzogchen, Kongtrul is referring to the mind series (*sems sde*).

181 See note 26.

182 Madhyamaka (*dbu ma*): the system expounded in the Mahayana sutras that teaches the emptiness of all phenomena. Here, however, Kongtrul is referring to the esoteric instructions stemming from that system more than the philosophical system itself.

Pacification (*zhi byed*) of suffering is a system of practice propagated in Tibet by the great Indian master Pha Tampa Sangye (eleventh/twelfth century).

Chöd (*gcod*) or *chöd yul* (*chod yul*) is an independent sytem of practice based on the integration of the principles of Sutra and Tantra developed in Tibet by the female master Machig Lapdrön (1055-1143).

183 *snying thig:* quintessential or heart essence, here a name for Dzogchen *upadesha*.

184 A lineage master of Atiyoga, Vimalamitra (ninth century) was a disciple of Shri Singha. He is particularly known for having transmitted in Tibet the series of secret instructions (*mang ngag sde*), subsequently codified as the *Vima snying thig*.

185 *rtsa dbu ma*; Skt. *madhyama:* The central channel, also referred to as *avadhuti*, originates from the power of the wind energy. It is known as central, or all--abandoning (*kun spangs ma*) because it is beyond the extremes of both the lunar and solar wind energies (that is, the karmic winds). When the wind energies that flow in the right and left channels enter and dissolve in it, the concepts of subject and object cease. Kongtrul explains it in the following way:

"A number of assertions about the central channel exist: that there are two types of central channel, the abiding one and the one imagined in meditation which is the assertion of the majority; that the central channel is actually the spinal cord; that it is only the thickness of a horsehair, located in the center of the spinal cord; that it does not exist in reality; and so forth. The perspective of the magnificent Rangjung Dorje is as follows: the central channel is located in the middle part of the body. It is the nonduality of the apprehended and apprehender and thus the indivisibility of method and wisdom." *The Treasury of Knowledge: Systems of Buddhist Tantra* pp.172-173.

In any case, when winds and mind dissolve in the central channel, concepts cease, giving rise to limpid, nonconceptual wisdom.

186 This is a reference to practices such as gazing directly at the sky (*nam mkha' ar gtad*) or gazing into the depths of the sea.

187 *khad chags pa*: possibly, the same as *mgo snyom*, even or unruffled.

188 *zung 'jug*: union. In the tantras this refers to the inseparability of the two truths: the relative truth represented by the practice of the self-induced blessing, which has the body manifest as the illusory body of the deity, and the ultimate truth represented by the mind entering its natural state through the practice of luminous clarity. Such union cannot be divided by concepts of relative and ultimate: of one taste, it is the inseparability of object (the supreme emptiness) and subject (the unchanging bliss), like water mixed with milk. Here, however, union refers primarily to the experience of natural awareness and emptiness.

189 Vajrasattva and other appellations also refer to the union of appearance and emptiness, natural awareness and emptiness, compassion and emptiness, and so forth. Vajrasattva and the other deities of the tantric pantheon signify the innate nature (*rang bzhin lhan skyes*), the single binding nature of all phenomena, the union of emptiness and compassion.

190 Nothingness (*med pa*), pervasiveness (*phyal ba*), oneness (*gcig*), self-perfectedness (*lhun grub*).

191 *Om A Hum*: The three letters that symbolize the Body, Voice, and Mind of all enlightened beings as well as the primordial condition of the three doors of body, voice, and mind of each individual.

192 *The Sutra of Remembering the Jewels* (*dkon mchog dran pa'i mdo*) consists of three short sutras. See Bibliography.

193 *lta ba bka' rtags phyag rgya bzhi*.

194 Jambhala: a prominent deity of wealth in the Buddhist tantric pantheon.

195 *chang bu*: a dough of barley flour squeezed between the fingers so that an imprint of the five fingers remains. It is then dedicated to the *yakshas*.

196 The custom of dedicating a pinch of food to the *yakshini* Haritaka (*'phrog ma*) originated in India at the time of the Buddha. Legend says that the *yakshini* Haritaka had five hundred children to whom she fed daily five hundred

human beings. One day Buddha Shakyamuni hid one of her children and released him on the condition that she promise not to kill anymore. The Buddha assured her that his followers would offer her and her class of beings a consecrated bit of food from their meals everyday.

197 *'jur gegs:* narrow larynx spirits, beings of the *preta* class (*'yi dwags;* Skt. *preta*) whose constricted larynxes makes it almost impossible for them to swallow food and drink. These spirits, very greedy in their former lives, continually suffer from extreme hunger and thirst. The custom of dedicating consecrated water to those spirits originated at the time of the Buddha. Once a few monks as they were begging saw a narrow larynx spirit that could not down either food or drink. When they inquired of the Buddha about the karma of this being, he told them that this spirit had been stingy in his past life and had given only water to others. Now he could only partake of pure water and nothing else. The Buddha advised his monks to wash their hands well and offer water empowered with mantras to relieve his suffering.

198 *kha 'bar ma:* Blazing Mouth, a queen of the *preta* class. It is said that when Ananda encountered this spirit who was spitting fire, the spirit told him that he would die within seven days and be reborn also as a *preta.* Ananda asked advice of the Buddha who told him to offer pure, consecrated water to Blazing Mouth and the spirits of her class in order to purify his karma. Thus the custom of offering water to the spirits of the blazing mouth class originated.

199 Padmasambhava, as he was known in Oddiyana, his birthplace in western India. See note 8.

200 *rtugs rje chen po:* an appellation of the bodhisattva Avalokiteshvara, symbol of compassion.

201 Om Mani Padme Hum.

202 *bar rlung:* intermediate wind, the experience resulting from the practice of vase-like breathing (Skt. *kumbhaka*) in which part of the wind energy of the inhaled breath is retained at the navel, while breathing continues normally. Chögyal Namkhai Norbu, oral communication.

203 *ka ti shel kyi rtsa chen mo:* great crystal *kati* channel, one of the five inner channels which are the luminosity of the five wisdoms that branch from the clear light of the heart. The channels can reveal and increase the practice of the four visions (*snang ba bzhi*). Specifically the crystal *kati* channel which connects the

heart to the eyes serves as the basis for the arising of the clear light of vision. Here, to open the great *kati* channel to the sky means to keep the eyes open and remain in the clear light of vision. See *Myriad Worlds, Buddhist Cosmology in the Abhidharma, Kalachakra, and Dzogchen.* Ithaca: Snow Lion Publications, pp. 225-227.

204   The letter *Hum* represents one's primordial state and visualizing it is a method to enter the contemplation of that state. Chögyal Namkai Norbu, oral communication.

205   *gdod ma'i rgyal sa:* the primordial kingdom: the original place of freedom, synonymous with the level of enlightenment called primordial purity.

206   "Clear away the stale breath" refers to the application of breathing exercises such as the ninefold purification breaths.

207   *rdo rje bzlas pa:* the *vajra* recitation, in which indirect breathing produces the sound of the three letters, exhaling with *Hum,* pausing with *Ah,* inhaling with *Om.*

208   According to the tantras, a healthy young person takes 21,600 breaths daily, each breath including inhalation, pause, and exhalation.

209   Dagpo or Dagpo Lhaje Sönam Rinchen (1079-1153) also known as Gampopa, was the foremost disciple of the yogin Milarepa and the founder of the Dagpo Kagyü school.

210   *'jam rlung:* a relaxed, nonforced way of using the breath.

211   *yid bzlas:* profound mental recitation. While within the state of contemplation one recites the mantra of a tantric deity such as Chakrasamvara, without emitting any sound. Chögyal Namkai Norbu, oral communication.

212   *rmi lam 'dzin pa:* recognizing a dream, that is, to know that one is dreaming while the dream occurs; transforming (*bsgyur ba*), to change the nature of the dream one is having; multiplying (*spel ba*), to increase the dream images. Purifying (*sbyang ba*): the training whereby a dream manifests as a deity and the dreamer, recognizing the unreal nature of this manifestation, remains in a state of bliss, emptiness, and luminous clarity.

213   *bar do chod pa:* cutting through the intermediate state, that is, recognizing that the visions one has during the intermediate state between death and rebirth are one's own manifestations.

214 *sgyu lus:* illusory body. This is tantric practice through which the practitioner actually manifests as the form and the mandala of the deity, and at the same time performs ordinary activities.

215 *spyod lam rnam bzhi:* the four activities of standing, walking, sitting, and lying down.

216 Shrimat: the name of the attendant of the fourteenth Karmapa cited in the colophon. The Sanskrit word *shrimat* means glorious (*dpal ldan*).

217 *bslab pa gsum:* training in ethics (*tshul khrims*), meditation (*ting nge 'dzin*), and wisdom (*shes rab*).

Index of Tibetan and Sanskrit Terms

'bras bu rdo rje 'dzin pa 108
'bur 'joms mgo thug 114
'du byed 114
'jur gegs 120
'phags lam yan lag brgyad 97
'du shes 114

a shad 100
Abhayākara 83
Abhidharma 88, 121
Amitābha, 'od dpag med 43
Ānanda, kun dga' 13, 120
Anuttara tantra 20, 21, 48, 104, 105
Anuyoga 19, 20, 22
Āryadeva, 'phags pa lha 13
Atiśa 75, 110
Atiyoga 19, 20, 65, 69, 94, 118
bali, gtor ma 71, 96
Bamten Trulku, bam steng sprul sku 13
bar do chod pa 121
bcos ma 102
bcos ma'i rnal 'byor 102
bden gnyis dyer med 116
bdud rtsi lnga 99

dri chu 99
dri chen 99
rak ta 99
byangs sems dkar po 99
rkang mar 99
bdud rtsi myong ba 99
bodhichitta, byang chub sems 20, 31, 49, 79, 116
Bokhar Rinpoche, 'bo dkar rin po che 9
brag cha 98
brdzus skyes 107
brtags pa'i rim pa 102
bsags sbyangs 102
bslab pa gsum 122
  tshul khrims 122
  ting nge 'dzin 122
  shes rab 122
bsnyen sgrub yan lag bzhi 103
bsnyen pa 103
nye ba'i bsnyen pa 103
grub pa 103
sgrub pa chen po 103
bsod nams bsags pa 96
Buddhaguhya 84, 113
Butön, bu ston 95

byang chub kyi phyogs kyi chos sum cu so bdun 97
byang chub kyi yan lag bdun 97

cāṇḍali, gtum mo 100
cakra, 'khor lo 31,
Cakrasaṃvara 44, 83, 94-97, 104, 121
caryātantra, spyod pa'i rgyud 20
chang bu 119
cho ga gsum 106
Chöd Yul, chod yul 118
Chöd, gcod 63, 118
Chogyur Lingpa, mchog 'gyur gling pa 15-17, 89, 94
chu nang gi gzugs brnyan 98
Cittamātra, sems tsam 112

dag pa dran pa 99, 111
Dagpo Lhaje Sönam Rinchen, dwags po lha rje bsod nams rin chen 121
Dagpo, dwag po 72, 121
ḍākinī, mkha' 'gro 70, 97, 101
dal 'byor rin chen 101
dbang po lnga 97, 115
dbang shes lnga 98
dbyibs kyi rnal 'byor 105
de ma thag pa'i yid 113
Derge, sde dge 11, 13, 17, 92
dharma, chos 37, 73, 80
dharmadhatu, chos dbyings 104, 113
dka' ba med pa 102
dkon mchog 82, 102, 119

dkon mchog gsum 102
do shal phyed 97
dran pa 82, 97, 99, 101, 111, 119
dran pa nye bar bzhag pa bzhi 97
drang ba'i lam 103
Drenthang, dren thang 18
dri za'i grong khyer 98
drod gsher skyes 107
drod rtags 115
Drugpa Kagyü 104
dur khrod brgyad 98
Dzogchen, rdzogs chen 15, 16, 18, 19, 31, 33, 52, 62, 63, 87, 88, 91-95, 117-118, 121
rdzogs chen sems sde 94, 117
rdzogs chen klong sde 94
rdzogs chen mang ngag sde 94, 118

gaṇacakra, tshogs kyi'khor lo 111
Gampopa, sgam po pa 91, 95
Garab Dorje 94,
gdangs 117
gdod ma'i rgyal sa 121
Gelug, dge lugs 12, 95
gnas lugs 102
gnyis sbyor gyi dga' ba bzhi 99
gtsag bu 107
guhyamantra, gsang ngags 104
Guru Padmasambhava, gu ru pad ma 'byung gnas 11, 12, 92, 95, 101, 120
Guru Rinpoche, gu ru rin po che 14, 15, 17, 92
guru yoga, bla ma'i rnal 'byor 71

Index of Tibetan Words and Terms

Gyalwa Götsangpa, rgyal ba rgod tshang pa mgon po rdo rje 104
Gyalwa Yangönpa, rgyal ba yang dgon pa 104
Gyurme Thutob Namgyal, 'gyur med mthu stobs rnam rgyal 12, 13, 92

heruka, he ru ka 23, 43, 44, 90, 94, 95, 96, 104
Hevajra 28, 81-86, 95, 98, 99, 102, 103, 105, 106, 109,

Jalandhara 83, 98
Jambhala, dzm bha la 71, 119
Jamgön Kongtrul Lodrö Taye, 'jam mgon kong sprul blo gros mtha' yas 9, 11-19, 33, 84, 88, 91, 92, 93, 95, 99-101, 103, 105, 106-111, 115, 116, 118
Jamyang Khyentse Wangpo, 'jam dbyangs mkhyen brtse'i dbang po 13-18, 89, 92, 93
Jigme Losal, 'jigs med blo gsal 11
jñānasattva, ye she se sems dpa' 110

ka dag 117
ka ti shel kyi rtsa chen mo 120, 121
Kadam, bka' gdams 18, 95
Kagyü, bka' brgyud 12, 13, 14, 18, 65, 85, 86, 91-96, 104, 113, 116, 121
Kama, bka' ma 12
Kamalarakṣita 83, 99

Karma Kagyü, kar ma bka' brgyud 13, 91

Karma Ngawang Yonten Gyatsho, kar ma ngag dbang yon tan rgya mtsho 74
Karma Palden, kar ma dpal ldan 19, 74, 101
Karmapa Tüsum Khyenpa, dus gsum mkhyen pa 11, 91
Karmapa Thegchog Dorje, kar ma pa theg mchog rdo rje 14, 93
Karmapa, kar ma pa 11, 14, 19, 74, 91-93, 101, 113, 122
kati 72, 120
kāya, sku 104
 dharmakāya, chos sku 32, 105, 108, 117
 saṃbhogakāya, longs sku 105, 108
 nirmāṇakāya, sprul sku 32, 104, 108, 117
 rupakāya, gzugs sku 105
 jñānakāya, ye shes chos sku 105
 svābhāvikakāya, ngo bo nyid sku 105
kha 'bar ma 120
khad chags pa 119
khams gsum 117
 'dod pa'i khams 117
 gzugs khams 117
 gzugs med khams 117
khrag 'thung 96
khu 109

Khyungpo Naljor, khyung po rnal 'byor 11, 13
Ko Dragpa Sönam Gyaltsen, ko brag pa bsod rnam rgyal mtshan 104
Kongpo, kong po 13
Kongtrul Lodrö Thaye, kong sprul blo gros mtha' yas 9, 11-19, 33, 84, 88, 91, 92, 93, 95, 99, 100, 101, 103, 105-111, 115, 116, 118
kriyātantra, bya ba'i rgyud 19
kun gzhi 113
kun gzhi rnam shes 98, 112, 115
kun gzhi ye shes 116
Kunzang Sang Ngag, kun bzang gsang sngags 12

Lama Wön, bla ma dbon 17, 18, 93
las su rung ba 115
len pa'i rnam par shes pa 113
lhag mthong 117
Lhawang Trashi, lha dbang bkra shis 9, 75
lhun grub 117, 119
lhun gyis grub pa'i rig 'dzin 111
Loden Nyingpo, blo ldan snying po 11, 91
Longdol Lama 86, 115
lta ba 102, 119
lta ba bka' rtags phyag rgya bzhi 119
lung du ma bstan pa 113
lus dang rtsa'i stong ra 100

Lvavapa 83

Machig Labdrön, ma gcig lab sgron 118
mādhyama, rtsa dbu ma 118
Mādhyamaka, dbu ma 63, 118
Mahāmudrā, phyag rgya chen po 19, 30, 33, 43, 45, 52, 62, 63, 87, 95, 99, 104, 116
Mahānuttara yogatantra 20
Mahāyāna, theg pa chen po 19, 49, 112, 118
Mahāyoga, rnal 'byor chen po 19, 20, 22, 60, 107,
maṇḍala, dkyil 'khor 7, 22, 23, 25,-27, 31, 38, 48, 49, 95, 96-101, 103, 106, 109-112, 116, 122
Mañjuśrīmitra 94
mantra, sngags 23, 24, 27, 41, 42, 43, 49, 65, 71, 72, 79, 85, 86, 89, 95-99, 102, 104, 105, 115, 120, 121
Marpa 15, 85, 90, 91, 93, 94, 95, 107
Matāṅgī, ma tang gi 97
mchog dang thun mong gi dngos grub 103
me long nang gi gzugs brnyan 98, 113
mgo snyom 119
mi sdug pa sgoms pa 104
mig rgyu 98, 114
Milarepa, mi la ras pa 11, 91, 121
mngal gyi gnas skabs lnga 108
mer mer po 108

ltar ltar po 108
gor gor po 108
mkhrang 'gyur 108
rkang lag 'gyus 108
mngal skyes 106
mngon byang lnga 105
mtshan dpe 105
mudrā, phyag rgya 97

nāḍi, rtsa 99
  lalanā, rkyang ma 30, 31
  rasanā, ro ma 30, 31, 115
  avadhūtī, kun spangs ma 118
nad 107
  tsha ba'i nad 107
  grang ba'i nad 107
nāga, klu 24, 98
Nāgārjuna, klu grub 39, 52, 93, 102
nam mkha' ar gtad 119
nges pa'i lam 103
ngo bo stong pa 117
niṣpannakrama, rdzogs rim 102
nirvāṇa 112
nyid 113
Nyingma, rnying ma 11, 12, 14, 18, 19, 20, 87, 90, 92-95, 107, 111,
nyon mongs kyi yid 98

Oddiyāna 71, 92, 94, 120

Padma Vajra, mtsho skyes rdo rje 37
Padmavajra 84, 113

Palpung, dpal spungs 12-14, 17, 18, 85, 86, 92, 96
pha skal phog 110
Pha Tampa Sangye, pha dam pa sangs rgyas 118
phyag rgya chen po'i rig 'dzin 111
phyag rgya chen po'i rnal 'byor bzhi 116
  rtse gcig 116
  spros bral 116
  ro gcig 116
  sgom med 116
pratyekabuddha, rang rgyal 19
Pukkasī 109

Rāhulaguyha 84, 97, 98
rang bzhin gsal ba 117
rang bzhin lhan skyes 119
Rangjung Dorje, rang byung rdo rje 85, 113, 115, 118
rdo rje bzhi 106
rdo rje bzlas pa 121
rdo rje mche po 101
rdul 109
rdzu 'phrul kyi rkang pa bzhi 97
reg pa 114
rgya che ba 102
rgyas bdag pa 54
rgyu rdo rje 'dzin pa 108
rig pa 100, 111, 116
rig pa 'dzin pa 86, 111
ril por 'dzin pa 100
rin chen gter mdzod 92, 94, 95
Rinchen Zangpo, rin chen bzang po 107

rjes su gzhig pa 100
rkang mgyogs 103
rlung 99, 108, 114, 115, 120, 121
  'jam rlung 121
  lha mo lnga'i rlung 115
  dbang po lnga'i rlung 115
  bar rlung 120
rlung bcu 114
  srog 'dzin 114
  thur du sel ba 114
  me dang mnyam du gnas pa 114
  gyen du rgyu ba 114
  khyab byed 114
  rgyu ba 114
  rnam par rgyu ba 115
  yang dag rgyu ba 115
  rab tu rgyu ba 114
  nges par rgyu ba 114
rmi lam 98, 121
  rmi lam 'dzin pa 121
  bsgyur ba 121
  spel ba 121
  sbyang ba 121
rmongs pa med pa 102
rnal ma 102
rnam dkar dge ba 113
rnam par smin pa'i rig 'dzin 111
rnam shes tshogs brgyad 112
  kun gzhi rnam shes 112
  nyon yid rnam shes 112
  yid kyi rnam shes 112
  sgo lnga'i rnam shes 112
  rnam smin 113
rol pa 117
rdul 108

rtags bcu 114
  du ba 114
  smig rgyu 114
  mkha'i snang 114
  sgron me 114
  'bar ba 114
  zla ba 114
  nyi ma 114
  rahu, sgra gcan 114
  kāla, cha/klog 114
  thig le chen po 114
rten 'brel 104
rten 'brel bcu gnyis 114
rten bzhengs pa 103
rtsal 117
rtsod dus 101
rtugs rje chen po 120
Rumtek 82, 85

sa, bhūmi·115, 121
saṃsāra 112
sadaṅgayoga 114
sādhana, sgrub thabs 25, 26, 47, 49, 96-99, 107, 109, 110
Sakya, sa skya 13, 15, 18, 93, 95
Samantabhadra, kun tu bzang po 20, 21
samayāsattva, dam tshig sems dpa' 110
Śāntideva, zhi ba'i lha 78
Śāntigupta 7
Sarma, gsar ma 20
Saroruha 110
sems nyid 113

Senge Namdzong, seng ge rnam
  rdzong 12
sgo gsum 101
sgom pa 102
sgon skyes 106
sgrib pa 105
  shes bya'i sgrib pa 105
  nyong rmongs pa'i sgrib pa 105
  snyoms 'jug gi sgrib pa 105
sgyu lus 122
sha lnga 99
  mi 99
  ba lang 99
  khyi 99
  rta 99
  glang po che 99
Shardza Trashi Gyaltsen, shar rdza
  bkra shis rgyal mtshan 91
Shechen, zhe chen 11-13, 92
shes bya kun khyab 85, 94, 95,
  107, 111, 113
shes bzhin 101
Shri Singha 118
siddha, grub thob 29, 91, 93, 94,
  98, 102
Situ Pema Nyinje Wangpo, si tu
  pad ma nyin byed dbang po 14,
  15, 17, 92, 93
skyabs su 'gro ba 97
smad lugs 92
sman 107
  bsil sman 107
  drod sman 107
sna tshogs rdo rje 96
snang ba bzhi 120

snang ba 109
snang ba mched pa 109
snang ba thob pa 109
'od gsal 109
snang ba dkar dmar 109
snang ba dkar lam pa 109
snang ba dmar lam pa 109
snyigs ma 101
snying thig 86, 94, 118
Sogdogpa Lodrö Gyaltsen, sog zlog
  pa blo gros rgyal mtshan 117
spyod lam rnam bzhi 122
spyod pa 100, 102,
śrāvaka, nyan thos 19
Śrīmat, dpal ldan 74, 122
srung du med pa'i dam tshig bzhi
  119
  med pa 119
  phyal ba 119
  gcig pu 119
  lhun grub 119
stegs bu 97
stobs lnga 97
stod lugs 93
stong pa 99, 102, 117
stūpa, dkyil 'khor 24, 103
sugatagarbha, bde gzhegs snying po
  104

Tai Situ 92
Tāranātha 13, 93, 105
Terdag Lingpa, gter bdag gling pa
  13, 92, 93
terma, gter ma 12, 14, 16, 17, 88,
  92, 94

tertön, gter ston 11, 15, 93, 94
tha mal shes pa 116
thabs lam 102
thabs mang ba 102
thams cad mkhyen pa 81, 99, 103
Tharde, thar bde 11
thig le 81, 99, 110
thugs rje'i rol pa rtsal 117
thur ma 107
ting nge 'dzin gsum 107
  de bzhin nyid kyi ting nge 'dzin 107
  kun tu snang ba'i ting nge 'dzin 107
  rgyu'i ting nge 'dzin 107
Trisong Deutsen, khri srong de'u btsan 92, 94
Tripiṭakamālā 102
Tsadra Rinchen Trag, tswa 'dra rin chen brag 14
Tsephel of Khangsar, khang gsar tshe 'phel 12
Tsering Töndrub, tshe ring don grub 17
Tsongkhapa, tsong kha pa 96
tshad med bzhi 109
tshe la dbang ba'i rig 'dzin 111

ubhayatantra, gnyis ka'i rgyud 19
upadesha 62, 63, 65, 94, 118
utpattikrama, bskyed rim 102

vajra, rdo rje 26, 29-32, 37, 50, 83, 85, 96, 97, 99-101, 103, 108, 109, 121

Vajradhāra, rdo rje 'chang 25, 44, 45, 48, 49, 74, 108, 109
Vajrasattva, rdo rje sems dpa' 28, 67, 97, 119,
Vimalamitra 17, 64, 86, 94, 118
Vinaya, 'dul ba 12, 13, 92

Wöngen Trulku, dbon rgan sprul sku 13, 17, 18, 93

Yakṣa, snod sbyin 24, 98, 119
Yakṣinī Harītaka, 'phrog ma 71, 119
yan lag bdun pa   phyag 'tshal ba 96
  sdig pa bshags pa 96
  mchod pa 96
  dge ba rjes su yi rangs pa 96
  chos kyi 'khor lo bskor ba bskul ba 97
  mya ngan las mi bda' bar gsol ba 'debs pa 97
  bsngo ba 97
yang dag pa'i spong ba bzhi 97
ye shes gsum 117
  ngo bo 117
  rang bzhin 117
  thugs rje 117
ye shes lnga 113
  me long lta bu'i ye shes 113
  mnyam nyid ye shes 113
  sor rtog ye shes 104, 113
  bya ba grub pa'i ye shes 113
  chos dbyings ye shes 104, 113

Yeshe Tsogyal, ye shes mtsho rgyal
    17, 87, 95
yi dwags, preta 120
yid 98, 112
yid bzlas 121

yoga tantra, rnal 'byor rgyud 19,
    20, 22
Yoginī Tantras 105
yongs grub 102
Yungdrung Phüntsog, g.yung drung
    phun tshogs 11
Yungdrung Tendzin, g.yung drung
    bstan 'dzin 11

zab pa 102
zhi byed 118
zhi gnas 117
zung 'jug 119